ORGANISING INNOVATION: A MANAGEMENT STUDY

ORGANISING INNOVATION:
A MANAGEMENT STUDY

ISHWAR DAYAL
Management Development
Institute, Gurgaon

CONCEPT PUBLISHING COMPANY, NEW DELHI 110059

ISBN 81-7022-368-7

First Published 1991

Published and Printed by
Ashok Kumar Mittal
Concept Publishing Company
A/15-16, Commercial Block, Mohan Garden
NEW DELHI-110059 (India)

Lasertypeset by
Microtech Advance Printing Systems (P) Ltd.
H-13, Bali Nagar
NEW DELHI-110015

To My Wife

Amrit Kala

PREFACE

India's contribution to science, technology and engineering is far below its capability. The results achieved in these areas are much below the level of available manpower and the institutional base created for the purpose. This book explores why the output of research and that of national level educational institutions is below the expected level, or low when compared with similar institutions abroad. I have not devised a yardstick to measure output but the heads of institutions and scientists whom I interviewed shared this feeling. The review committees for the Council of Scientific and Industrial Research that accounts for bulk of expenditure on research, and similar bodies for technical education, have endorsed this view. We have to reflect on the reasons for this failure so that corrective measures can be taken to reverse the trend in future. My analysis is confined to managerial aspects of innovative institutions and not policy or macro level issues.

I have referred to these institutions as innovative because they are set up to innovate, to generate new knowledge and new applications of knowledge with the hope that these together will contribute effectively to solve the nation's economic and social problems. For this book I have visited 15 institutions and held indepth discussions with chief executives and a large sample of scientists. I have also relied on my own experience of twenty years in directing positions, and earlier as a teacher and researcher.

The experience of serving on the directing Boards of several institutions has also provided useful material for this volume. In the strictest sense this book is not a report of a research study, but it is based on data derived from the sources mentioned above. The book is based on experiences of other people and my own and not on data from a rigidly followed research study.

The purpose of this book is to identify areas that make innovative institutions ineffective. The articulation of problem areas at the institutional level is necessary for such organisations to deal with them. It is possible that some readers may consider additional problem areas and I hope they would be brought out. I would, however, emphasise that the problem of low performance is not due to lack of leadership but to a combination of factors that are identified here.

The book emphasises the processes that make institutions dysfunctional, and not the rational or the extant system which may govern the administration. The role of the Board of Governors, the Government and other related institutions may be conceived well or poorly in a project report: what's important is to see how they influence the internal systems of work. I have examined the process because the process of management helps us understand where things go wrong and how they may be set right. I hope students of management, administrators and managers of innovative institutions will find the analysis of the process useful.

Being a student of socio technical systems, I have examined the requirements of the task system and social organisation needed to harmonise it. I have also surveyed the essential characteristics of the management of innovative organisations in Western countries to show how such systems develop and become effective. I have also suggested some steps that we would have to take to make our innovative institutions more effective.

I am grateful to my colleague Vijay Aggarwal for comments on an earlier draft, and to K.V.L.N. Murty for typing the draft patiently.

New Delhi
May, 1991

ISHWAR DAYAL

CONTENTS

1

INTRODUCTION

I have examined in this book questions like, What are the factors that make many Indian scientists and teachers do better in foreign lands than they do in their own country? How educational and research institutions can become more effective. After all, the contribution of these institutions is crucial to harnessing science and technology for development. We would have to use *knowledge* to improve our capability to effectively compete with the developed countries.

Industrial research in India began in 1940 with the creation of the Board of Scientific and Industrial Research. By a resolution of the Ministry of Commerce in 1942, Council for Scientific and Industrial Research (CSIR) was created. CSIR had the mandate to establish its own research institutions with responsibility for "the promotion, guidance and co-ordination of scientific and industrial research in India, including the financing of specific researchers". The constitution of CSIR provides periodical review of its work. So far four review committees have been set up in the years 1947, 1954, 1963 and 1986. All the committees have repeatedly expressed dissatisfaction with the overall performance of the CSIR System. The 1986 Review Committee headed by Abid Hussain lists out the following among its major failures:

- CSIR System has made useful contributions but has not provided much in terms of scientific breakthroughs or advances in the frontiers of knowledge which have received international recognition.
- It has been unable to develop technologies which would meet even the most agonising needs of our economy and society, let alone facilitate modernisation.
- There are vast variations in the calibre of scientists in different labs which does not always conform to standards of excellence.
- There is no clear sense of direction. The major failure is its inability to transform results in the labs into technologies for industrial production.
- Disproportionate emphasis is placed on work on known products and processes.

As the present study shows, these conclusions are generally applicable to most research and educational institutions and not CSIR laboratories alone.

I have tried to identify critical problems that impede growth of institutions in India, and have suggested areas of improvement and a strategy. The right answers will come only through experimentation and a firm desire on the part of decision-makers to enhance our capability for achieving better results. Institutional management would also have to make conscious efforts to identify and overcome factors that prevent them to serve the intended purpose, and improve productivity.

In India market forces are not powerful enough to induce the need for change in the internal management system of institutions. At times a sense of personal responsibility induces organisational leadership to take up a programme of change. In some cases, public opinion and parliamentary strictures induce re-thinking on the performance of an organisation. But these pressures are not as powerful as the market forces induced by competition, or the need for survival. Hence organisational change in most cases is self-induced and depends primarily on the urges of a few people at decision-making levels.

The other inhibition to improving effectiveness is the tolerance of low standards of performance and, using Gunnar Myrdal's term, a tendency for soft options.

Yet another factor that makes change difficult is the culture-bound behaviour of the people. The self-centredness, high control-orientation, low tolerance of ambiguity, dependency needs and the like which become dysfunctional for managing large organisations. These aspects have been highlighted in behavioural research and in studies of how large organisations are managed (Sinha, 1977; Chattopadhyay, 1980; Dayal, 1977). The essential disposition of management is common to organisation in the public, the private and the government alike. Changes in organisational practices and in the behaviour of people in it need both systemic and behavioural changes. Hence, organisational development programmes have to be concerned with several related aspects: the understanding of behaviour in organisations, the leadership and the organisation of the work and related issues (Whyte, 1969; Dayal, 1970).

Several of the organisational change programmes undertaken in India are impressive. But, the process of change is complex and time-consuming. This is so because on the one hand the change required is transition from agrarian to industrial value system, and on the other there is inadequate experience of managing complex organisations as current experience is often confined to managing small organisations. Further, commitment of time on the part of top and senior management and dedication to the idea of changing organisational culture is a necessary condition for success of such programmes. Most successful programmes of this nature have taken three to five years of intensive work to achieve positive results. Such programmes are not a one-time effort; they require almost continuous attention of top management.

In government also many impressive changes have been made. The experience of large-scale reforms in the management of government have, however, met with limited success both in the developed and the developing countries. The impact of the massive exercise in reforms in India by setting up the Administrative Reforms Commission (1966 - 69) is hardly noticeable. The impact of the much talked about Fulton Committee Report (Garret, 1972) in Great Britain has also been somewhat limited. However, some programmes of improvement in Australia, Canada and the U.K. under Mrs. Margaret Thatcher are reported to have been successful.

The book analyses the task characteristics of innovative institutions and discusses their administrative implications. In one essential respect this book differs from those that hold inadequacy of leadership as responsible for ineffectiveness of organisations (Singh and Bhandarkar, 1990). The leader alone cannot sustain the quality or effectiveness of an institution. It needs the support of the factors that critically influence its working. The most important of these factors are the nature of the controlling authority, the people within the institution and the governing board. Individuals can influence the direction, and they may protect the institution from negative controls for a period of time, but such influence is unlikely to build up an institution. Homi Bhabha and Vikram Sarabhai, for instance, were able to provide positive leadership to the atomic research programme but this was possible only because they had the direct support of the Prime Minister, and therefore the government, which enabled them to minimise the influence of negative control. I believe leaders will be attracted to lead institutions, and are likely to be effective, when systemic changes accompany positive leadership interventions. We have had outstanding leaders, but their influence on institutions has been temporary. Improvement in the output of institutions requires pains taking systemic and behavioural changes and not individual leadership alone. This book deals mainly with the systemic and behavioural changes that are needed to make institutions effective.

The data for this book are obtained principally from four sources: (i) interviews with 15 chief executives of educational and research institutions and about 30 teachers and researchers, (ii) as consultant to several institutions, (iii) as member of review committees, and (iv) personal experience in India and abroad. But, strictly, this book is not a research report, though it is based on the data obtained from the sources mentioned here.

2

THE FRAMEWORK

Analysis of an organisation needs a framework. In this study the concept of socio-technical system is used. The harmony between the requirements of the task system and the social organisation of work are necessary for an organisation to be productive. The analysis of the innovative organisations is based on five basic requirements of the organisation. The characteristics of these are discussed below:

(i) The work organisation or socio-technical system
(ii) The concept of autonomy
(iii) The concept of standardisation
(iv) The concept of power or politicisation
(v) The concept of equilibrium or balance

(i) The Socio-technical System

Harmony between the requirements of the task, referred to as technology, and the social organisation of work is necessary. Different task systems need different kinds of social organisation, and an administrative system to suit the situation. Let us consider two educational institutions, a social science faculty in a university and an institution for professional education, say, a management school. The social science faculty is concerned with advancement of knowledge in a discipline. The management school is concerned with how best knowledge can be used to improve our understanding of a situation, and in evaluating alternative choices of action for best possible results. The discipline-based research and teaching will need computing facilities, library and interaction among those who speak the same language. The management researcher will need different kinds of support systems such as liaison with work organisations, scope for discussion with persons from many other areas, each having a different language, a more interactive relationship with computer and library. The social organisation of the management school will need a far greater measure of interdependence among support service personnel and researchers than the social science faculty. The kind of people who will be attracted to the two institutions will have distinct interests and the persons who provide support services would have different functions to perform. The nature of job in the business school would require greater physical space to facilitate interaction, provide travel facilities and greater encouragement to try out ideas in the laboratory, i.e. business organisations. The mix of activities in terms of teaching, research and experimentation would be different from one person to another and from one period to another for the same person. Hence it would need a work planning system for each faculty member.

Briefly, the two tasks require different approaches in respect to the following:

(a) Conscious development of social organisation of work groups to facilitate interactions among them. Where greater interdependence and social interaction among researchers and support services staff is needed, the hierarchy would have to be the minimum, the mutual respect among members should be high and interaction should be easy.

(b) The nature of responsibility in two systems will be different for the operating people. The researcher, the liaison and the support services staff will have to perform multiple roles and they must all show appreciation for each other's roles.

(c) The travel rules, procedures for sanction, review procedures in two situations will be different. In a management school the procedures will have to be simple and allow for flexibility. In another institution the need for these may not be as great.

In management school, individuals have to volunteer for tasks that interest them. Each project has unique requirements. Projects may require consultation or collaboration with other persons or institutions. Some others may require travelling. The support staff requirements would vary from one project to another. The field staff may have different requirements.

The administrative arrangements would have to be flexible so that the requirements of equipment, staff, etc., can be met without losing time in pushing papers from one desk to another. In most institutions, the procedures set out for services are exasperating. There are many persons who bear the cost themselves to avoid filling up forms. The travel is put on other than institutional account because the rules disallow such expenses, though legitimate. The administrative staff literally follow the rules and show least concern for the requirements of the project. Invariably the scientist has to approach the Chief Executive for accommodation.

Admitted, institutions cannot function without rules and regulations, but these should be the minimum possible. An institutional management would have to exercise discretion in many more situations in the school of management than the department of social science in a university. The differences will be even more marked between an innovative organisation and an office which has repetitive work such as a manufacturing or an administrative unit.

It would be seen that the requirements of a post-graduate teaching and research institution are different from those of a Government office. Rules and regulations generally dominate the Government system where tasks should do. The social system of the innovative organisation would be different from that of a primarily administrative organisation.

(ii) The Concept of Autonomy

No position or person can have total freedom of action, or total autonomy. A manager must, however, have discretion to decide on those aspects which significantly influence achievement of results. Assuming a Production Manager is required to give a product of a certain quality, at a certain cost and on an agreed schedule, he would be able to achieve these results if he could exercise discretion in respect to maintenance, manpower and production scheduling which critically influence quality, cost and output. To the extent he is not able to exercise discretion or judgement in respect to these critical elements of the production process, he may not be able to achieve the results. Hence, autonomy for a production manager requires that he should be able to exercise discretion in areas that are critical for achieving the desired results.

The manager of an innovative system can achieve results if he can generally exercise discretion in respect of the management of institutional tasks, selection of work teams, assess performance and exercise control over resources needed to provide the required facilities for good work. The institutional management should have total discretion to manage the agreed programmes within the limits set for the purpose by the governance system. Thus autonomy is related to the task that a manager is required to perform. It is not a favour bestowed on the individual but an essential condition for a position to achieve the expected results. The role incumbent must be able to exercise his judgement in those aspects of work that significantly influence results. The chief executive of an institution must have control over people, finances and such other elements as influence results. Operationally the governing system therefore should define the programmes and the expected level of results and approve resources needed to carry out the tasks, and having done so, the institutional management should exercise discretion for managing the programmes. If the discretion is curtailed, then the person concerned or the institution will have curtailed autonomy, and he may not be able to achieve the expected results.

The Abid Hussain Review Committee Report (p. 42) comments:

> "CSIR was intended to function as an autonomous society. However, it has not taken advantage of this. Even as early as 1966 Homi Bhabha had pointed out that the opportunity of framing an administrative structure and rules and procedures appropriate for a scientific organisation which a society-type set-up was intended to confer on CSIR has been lost by the omnibus adoption of government-like rules and regulations."

The adoption of structures and procedures has not been an option of the institution. The way in which government-like rules and regulations enter an institution, and hold it, is the concern of this volume.

(iii) The Concept of Standardisation

Rules and regulations should facilitate performance of work. But in many institutions they hinder rather than help people engaged in serious work. The consequent negative effects of such inhibitive rules are handled by institutions in many ways. In some institutions an informal understanding is developed to ignore certain rules because without bypassing them, institutional tasks cannot be performed. Those employees who develop expertise in devising methods of bypassing hard rules gain importance in the organisation irrespective of their rank or status. One senior officer was in the habit of asking his superior what is it that he desired done and he would prepare a note to do precisely that. He had acquired the ability to interpret rules to fit the decision. He belonged to a group of people in rule-bound organisations who learn the art of mastering the rules. Such persons often excel in a bureaucracy and are generally in great demand. Commenting on public administration, Jawaharlal Nehru says, ". . . the test of an administration is not some paper rules and regulations aiming at perfection but the actual performance. It is better to make mistakes occasionally but the greater mistake is to pursue methods which delay" (Saxena, 1990, p. 95).

Rules must suit the situation for which they are framed. A research organisation, for example, invariably requires travel for long periods at a time as interviews have to be held according to the needs of the project or the client organisation. A business organisation requires short visits to complete a finite task. Travel rules of one organisation cannot suit the other. In this way rules must facilitate task performance, not block it.

When rules of one organisation are imposed on another which has a totally different task system, the receiving organisation will experience difficulty in operating them. It will not be able to develop a pattern of interactions, or work culture best suited to its own requirements. The standardisation imposed upon it by the host organisation will in this sense be dysfunctional.

Many practices or rules are formulated as a part of the organisation's history. Some practices develop while solving individual problems and issues. In some cases precedence becomes a rule, however, inappropriate the practice might be. If these practices are imposed upon another institution which has a different history, or circumstances, then it is called *standardisation* in this book.

The Government has to deal with a large number of employees, and rules are made keeping this circumstance in view. To deal with the variety and size it has devised cadres, hierarchy, manning formulaes, qualifying requirements in respect to certain benefits, etc. The same practices may not be appropriate for another organisation which is much smaller, or does work that is totally different from that of the Government. The Government system is based on the classical assumptions of Weberian bureaucracy such as rational-legal approaches to work, impersonality in dealing with issues and rules governing work and relationships. If these practices are imposed upon a smaller institution which has different task requirements, it will be seen as standardisation. Some provisions are made because the country's Constitution provides certain safeguards or benefits for all its citizens. These have to be followed and cannot be seen as standardisation. Hence standardisation is one where certain practices are imposed upon one organisation even when the requirements of that system are different. To take a simple example, the TA/DA rules for Government organisations are framed on the basis that they are provided accommodation at highly subsidised rates. The same cannot apply to an autonomous institution which has no guest house or subsidised accommodation. So, if the Government practice is applied to another institution which operates on considerations different from those of the Government, the approach will be termed as *standardisation*. And when such a "standardisation" is imposed upon an institution, the employees of the institution concerned will have to stop travelling or suffer financial loss or manipulate the TA/DA account. The standardisation will be dysfunctional for the institution because the practice that is suitable for one system, when applied to another, fails to serve its particular purpose. At the same time if the Constitution or any other law of the country gives certain privileges to an employee, any regulation to safeguard such privileges will have to be observed. Any rule or regulation formulated to follow this requirement, whether it suits the institutional task or not, cannot be considered as standardisation.

The administrative practices are meant to facilitate work, and they should smoothen the work flow. As in the above example of TA/DA, if employees are not able to travel because going out would mean going out of pocket, the basic activity such as field-based research will suffer and institutional management will not be able to encourage research staff to undertake such work. In one organisation dealing with applied areas of study

I found research studies included mainly library work. This institution followed Government of India rules which stipulated that anycne who remains on tour for more than 10 days will be eligible for only a portion of the TA/DA. As research work involved absence for longer periods at a time, the research staff over time avoided projects that required absence for longer periods in the field. The scientists took up library projects, and once this tradition was set up, researchers interested in projects with application bias did not come to the institution. Hence the institution became known only for certain kinds of projects. The image of the institution was established by the kind of research publications it had. The standardisation, as in this case, was dysfunctional, i.e. adversely affected the purpose for which the institution was set up.

The example of TA/DA is meant only to be an illustration to explain how an inappropriate rule influences performance. The shift in the focus of research in the above example was reinforced by many other practices as well. The institution valued the number of publications, and library research helped the faculty to churn out more written output than they could on the basis of field studies. In this institution intellectual work or pure research was valued more than application-oriented research. The faculty felt proud of their links with university departments than with work organisations. All these factors combined gave the institution its character. The institutional management was, however, unable to change this trend due to the limitation of TA/DA as the Government disallowed the proposed change.

Standardisation, as would be clear, has two serious difficulties. One, the rule interpreter, the administrator becomes a central figure in the life of the institution, and being so, acquires power over people.

Two, the researcher develops an attitude which says, "Would rules allow me to take up this work?" rather than, "This is an interesting problem and I must seek out people who will collaborate with me".

Invariably the researcher has to fill up a large number of forms in multiple copies for incurring any expenditure even before an idea has matured into a researchable proposition. What is regrettable is that most people in organisations become so conditioned by the system that they are uncomfortable without such procedures.

(iv) The Concept of Power or Politicisation

The phenomenon of politicisation occurs when a decision is taken to suit the interests or convenience of another organisation than the one where a problem has arisen which requires that decision. If a case of indiscipline has occurred in organisation "A" and the decision to deal with that situation is taken because organisation "B" is likely to face the problem, that decision is seen here as a political decision. Often political decisions in an organisation become necessary. At times the repercussions of a decision on, say, organisation "B", which is a strategic organisation, may be comprehensive and the decision to compromise in organisation "A" may be prudent, or desirable. No value is attached to politicisation except that such a decision has repercussions in organisation "A". If a large number of decisions in "A" are political in nature, the organisation is likely to lose its autonomy. In such an eventuality the local management would not be able to exercise managerial controls.

(v) The Concept of Equilibrium or Balance

Organisations are subject to multiple forces at any given point of time. Lewin has promoted the idea of force field for understanding a problem as it applies to mechanics in the study of physics. The operative aspect of the concept is that a particular situation can be explained by a balance of a variety of forces operating in the situation. Like the solar system, the position "S" is caused by a balancing of multiple forces, and therefore what may appear to be a static position in fact represents dynamic forces, which at that point in time are balanced. The implication is that change in the potency of any force will disturb the equilibrium and cause imbalance in the total system, and not in the sub-system where the particular force is exerted. This phenomenon may best be explained by an example. Sales at 100 units may express a particular level of effort on the part of the sales staff, the production people, the product design people, the employee skills and many such factors. Enhanced level of employee skills may change the balance. The product quality may improve, new market may develop, and the sale may go up from 100 to 125 units. A new equilibrium would have to be achieved where the sales people may have to give more energy, the design people may have to produce a better product and contribute to the establishment of a new balance. Also, change in enhanced skills has its impact on several other sub-systems besides the production system. This being the reality, an organisational situation is better understood in terms of the concept of equilibrium rather than the Newtonian concept of balance being achieved by a set of equal and opposite forces.

The five aspects of an organisation discussed here are useful for analysing the dynamics of an organisation. They provide minimum conditions for the organisation to remain active. This framework may not, and it is not meant to be, comprehensive or exclusive for analysing an organisation.

3

THE PROCESS

Output of most institutions in India can at best he classified as mediocre when compared to the expenditure incurred on them or the quality of the manpower available to them. Some institutions show periods of high performance but it is rare for anyone to maintain output of a consistently high quality. There are many institutions which never perform the tasks at the level expected of them. By and large most educational and research (innovative) institutions approach mediocrity when their performance is measured against promise, or when compared with similar organisations in the developed countries. The CSIR Review Committee chaired by Abid Hussain had also come to similar conclusions in respect to their performance.

Low productivity is not always a function of the individual as a person. We have many individuals who have performed creditably abroad but have shown low output in India. The phenomenon has to be understood rather in the interaction between the individual and the situation in which he operates. The same individual is productive at one time in a given situation and he is average in another. Two statements from my interviews will illustrate the point. In sentiment these statements are not atypical of the people interviewed.

A scientist said,

> "I spent two months of the summer vacation in a university abroad, and I was able to do more work during this period than I have been able to do in the last two years here."

A medical doctor who came back after a Ph.D. on cancer studies abroad said,

> "It has taken me two years to set up a research project which would have taken no more than two weeks in the university abroad, and even now I have to fill up many gaps and chase some more people."

Three different kinds of factors contribute significantly to the output of scientists. These are:

(i) Environmental factors that condition patterns of work.
(ii) Internal management systems or the leadership that motivate people to give their best performance.
(iii) Quality of the scientist.

In the analysis in this book the factors that significantly influence the first and second aspects are analysed more fully than the third. The reason for taking this approach is that without the overall environmental or contextual factors, work systems suitable for task performance will be difficult to develop. The context factors provide the foundation for appropriate system to be developed in the institution.

The three contributory factors that constitute the context for most institutions in my sample, and also experience are:

(i) The Government in its entrepreneurial role.
(ii) The Governance system in its directional role.
(iii) The employee culture in its socialisation role.

The three systems being interdependent cumulatively contribute to the ineffectiveness of an institution. The analysis shows that the three systems in sum cause imbalance in the institutional management by politicisation of decision-making, by standardisation and by denial of autonomy in the functioning of the institution. This chapter discusses the dynamics, or the process, through which system dysfunctionality is caused.

Most educational and research organisations are funded by the Government in this country, hence the dynamics of its influence on lack of autonomy and standardisation, and its role in the governing system of the institution is critical.

The analysis emphasises that three systems—the Government, the governance and the employee expectations—induce forces that contribute to the development of an inappropriate administrative system in educational and research institutions. The role of each of the three is discussed individually before the measures to improve them are later considered.

Role of the Government

The Government creates new institutions to serve identified purposes. The achievement of this purpose by each institution will ultimately contribute towards improvement of the quality of life of the people. Viewed thus, each institution has a unique or distinctive contribution to make. What are the implications of this requirement for the management of the institution which in set up to produce a unique product?

The Dynamics of Standardisation

The terms of grant-in-aid require that salary grades, service conditions, classification of jobs, manning, etc., are similar in all aided institutions. When any point is raised by any institution the criterion used for decision by a Ministry in the Government is whether similar positions or practices exist in other organisations or not, and not whether the task system of the particular organisation justifies it. The rules are often compared with the rules prevailing in the Government of India, where the Civil Service Code is seen to serve as a norm.

Because funds are provided by the Government and the institution is an instrument of the Government with similar service rules and conditions, the courts of law have decreed that such institutions meet the definition of a State. The implication of this decision is that the considerations that apply to employment in the Government will also apply to such institutions. Most institutions are registered under the Societies Act with the intention that the Board of Governors will exercise the discretion in managing it in the best way suited to it. The Court decision apparently alter this consideration.

The standardisation is achieved by the system of approving the service rules by the Ministry. On all essential respects they have to be similar to those in Government. The employees in institutions prefer to have rules that apply to Government employees because they are liberal and they feel honoured emotionally to belong to what is generally referred to as Government service.

When rules become the central focus of administration the institutions have to employ someone who can understand these rules and interpret them in a uniform way. As the institution begins to function through the framework of rules, the employees react the way the practices assume they would—in the legal-rational frame. In this situation seniority, officiating allowance, hierarchy rather than merit, self-reliance, collaboration, etc. become the guidelines for behaviour. Performance evaluation, reward and punishment for good work or poor, resources development, etc., are replaced by normal grade increments, time-bound promotions, elaborate disciplinary rules and the like. The administrative practices so instituted are not a function of the task system but that of the generalised pattern born out of the compulsions of a very large and impersonal system whose work is different from that of the innovativc institution. Ironically, autonomous organisations are created to perform tasks that required different organisational practices but over time, they operate much the same way as the Government system does, or all other institutions do.

As the Government controls mainly expenditure and service rules and rarely results, standardisation makes it easier for the Government to exercise control. When the same practices apply to all institutions, decisions became easy. Comparison with other institutions and not the unique requirements of an institution form the core elements of decision-making in Government. Many matters have to be referred to the Ministry for clarification of rules. References are made on specific rules and on individual cases. More staff is needed in the Ministry and in the institution, and in other Ministries because references in many cases have also to be made from one Ministry to another. Notwithstanding the provision of the Act that the Board of Governors provide the direction and control of such "autonomous" bodies, in operating matters the institutions are perceived more as attached offices and less as autonomous bodies. In fact the Board is a formality; the Ministry has the directing role in matters of finance and administration.

The Dynamics of Autonomy

Autonomy as defined here is the necessary condition for a system to be effective. The management of the institution must be able to take decisions that would (a) achieve results expected of it and (b) develop patterns of interaction that would motivate people to achieve results. The question is how does the management integrate individual and institutional goals towards a common purpose.

In an ideal sense the chief executive creates a network of work roles, appoints people to manage the sub-systems within their role boundaries, provides policy direction, develops a planning, review and feedback system for various units and the overall system, and performs a leadership or impresario function to enthuse people to set high performance goals and achieve them. It is good to have an overall managerial view as this. In fact this picture does not exist in any organisation. Tasks are not fully performed by departments or individuals. Sub-goals of departments often become more important than organisational goals. Individuals and groups compete with other individuals and groups. The communication between units is distorted and the receiver is open to misinterpretation of the sender's intent, leading further to poorer inter-personal and inter-group relationships. The affiliations, interest groups, cabals and patterns that are found in the wider society also develop in the organisation. Rationality in dealing with one another has to be developed through conscious effort, and is not an attribute or a condition of social organisations. A coalition of diverse goals and purposes has to be developed to create an institutional identity. Hence the effectiveness of the organisation depends greatly on the top management's ability to achieve a balance between multi-directional and multi-dimensional forces in the environment.

The magnitude of these problems differs from one organisation to another, but in essence the socio-political environment of the organisation often has these features. Hence autonomy for institutional management must include effective management of socio-political besides task-related aspects of the system.

Generally autonomy is seen in terms of financial and administrative powers. The instruments of delegation are drawn up on the basis of the ideas mentioned earlier, e.g. the chief executive will perform within the framework of the policy and achieve through people results expected of the institution. In fact such powers only help in the carrying out of the "formal" transactions of the organisation. The overall system management depends on the network of influence or power relationships that exist between the executive system, the governing system and the power centres within and outside the organisation. Let me give from my sample a couple of live examples of these interactions and power relationships to illustrate the point made here.

* Within the Governing body of the institution an identifiable group based on service affiliations had been formed. No individual member gained from this membership except that the group as a whole, and members belonging to it, were able to influence decisions. The group became a power centre in the governing system. The chief executive of the institution found himself

open to three distinct kinds of pressure groups: (i) the group referred to above, i.e. the service group, (ii) the faculty and staff who formed an important part of the academic consultative bodies but not members of the governing body, and (iii) members of the governing body who did not belong to the service group. The members who belonged to the service group strengthened their position by encouraging members of the staff to provide information and they in turn represented and tacitly supported their representations in the governing body. Invariably staff members who did poorly and needed favours became the link with members of the service group. This transactional relationship gave the group further reinforcement to make it more cohesive. As this pattern became recognised by employees, the decision-making on personnel matters became extremely difficult within the institution and in the meetings of the governing body.

* In another institution the chief executive spent a great deal of his time in building relations with important persons who could help him in his career. He invited them to the institution for lectures even when such persons had limited contribution to make to the academic work of the institution. The faculty were neglected and the overall work of the institution suffered in terms of research, publication and quality of teaching. The faculty felt that they had little freedom in organising programmes that they formally headed. Two groups slowly emerged: one group close to the chief executive and one that disfavoured the infringement on academic work.

Autonomy is a wider concept than giving financial and administrative powers. It has to have an overall enabling concept to deal with the social and political system of the institution. The concept of autonomy must include two aspects: (i) authority or power needed to facilitate task performance and these are generally referred to as financial and administrative powers; (ii) enabling authority and powers that allow the chief executive to deal with the socio-political system. The first aspect is handled well enough by most institutions. The second is generally developed through conventions. The decision-making bodies will have to recognise the role boundary of the chief executive and generally deal with overall policy and direction and not individual cases. The power of influence centres residing outside the designated positions within the institution tend to compromise the authority of the management. In the first example the service group neglected the authority of the chief executive. The problem-solving mechanisms such as internal committees lost their useful and the system was rendered incapable of performing its functions. In the second example the chief executive assumes near absolute powers. The teachers performed a marginal role as members of the institution. The quality of work suffered due to total disregard of the requirements of the task system by the chief executive. The organisation must have countervailing authority for key positions, preferably within the framework of the managing system. These mechanisms enable the institution to develop rationality by effectively dealing with the prevailing political processes.

Experience in India has been that chief executive have been dictatorial or totally ineffective. The balance is difficult to achieve for yet another reason. This matter will be discussed in the section on the nature of employee culture. The employees are generally unable to accept the role boundary and exercise the maturity to differentiate between work and social roles. Acceptance of social reality in most cases is poor.

An Enabling Concept

Briefly then, the autonomy needed for institutional management is an enabling concept – it enables the institutional management to perform the tasks in the best possible way and for managing the socio-political environment. Brown (1971) has suggested that ideally power and authority should converge in the same position in the organisation. Power is concerned with influencing other people to behave in the desired direction and authority is an attribute of the position required for achieving the desired results. It should at least be possible for an institutional management to identify power centres which have the potential of disturbing the balance of forces within the organisation and effectively deal with them.

4

THE GOVERNANCE SYSTEM

The governance system, Board of Governors (BOG), invariably has two or three ex-officio seats. These are meant for the donor agency; in most institutions this agency is the Ministry. One seat is meant for the Financial Adviser of the Ministry or his nominee. The original idea of having ex-officio members was that they should provide a link between BOG and the Ministry. By knowing the Board's wish the members will be able to facilitate decision-making interface areas with the Ministry. Where individuals occupying the link position are perceptive, the system operates reasonably well. When such positions are occupied by persons who have a self-centred approach, the system experiences stresses and strains. In either case decisions can at best be compromises. The idea of a link position is based on two considerations:

(i) Since the Government has to be involved in major decisions, it is better to involve concerned people from the Ministry at the Board of Governors level.

(ii) As managers are meant to be rational beings and the two systems function on rational criteria, BOG and the Ministry can be usefully served by persons who are placed in link positions.

The bureaucracy takes a primarily rational view of decision-making and under-emphasises the socio-political processes in decision-making in organisations.

The Social System

Innovative institutions tend to develop a collegiate and consultative style because the nature of their work requires open peer relations and candid culture. For such a system to work well, employees have to show self-direction, result orientation, a sense of responsibility and respect for the ideas of other people. The maturity needed for an open system to work well has to be consciously developed because our child-rearing practices do not generally induce such behaviour. Studies show that feelings of inadequacy, hostility to the environment, extreme dependence, comfort with patronage, immediate gratification of one's perceived needs are the common patterns of normal behaviour (Kakar, 1971, 1970; Sinha, 1974; Whiting, 1968; Carstairs, 1957). Chattopadhya (1980) has emphasised that child-rearing practices in Indian middle class families develop strong feelings of rejection and guilt, and children are unable to develop a distinct identity. As adults, it is often difficult to cope with authority and these patterns contribute towards the lack of adjustment in organisations. It has been pointed out that many of these patterns of behaviour show up in organisations (Dayal, 1977). Because of the feelings of inadequacy and extreme dependence on authority, a sense of inadequacy, etc., the employees seem to need a high degree of structure, rules, direction and control. Many seek security in having an increased number of rules and regulations, and believe that they are essential conditions for a rational management system. In fact, a greater amount of manipulation, managing through patronage, etc., become necessary because the complicated and unsuitable structure of rules often prevents people from performing their roles effectively.

Most institutions start with minimum rules, feeling that issues should be decided on merit and not on the basis of a universal rule. But, seeing that every decision leads to grievances, representations, endless discussions, more rules are made to cover new situations. As rules are added, employees come with requests that exception should be made in their case. In many cases these are the same persons who had clamoured for additional rules. As the system becomes more rule-bound the administrative personnel at junior levels are added to examine each case in the light of the rules. With this the process of bureaucratisation begins. The decision-maker must also have information on past decisions – precedence and rules applicable in the case. A note has to be initiated invariably at lower levels of the office heirarchy and those who become *pundits* in the interpretation of rules develop vested interest in complicating them more and more. The stage is thus set for the pattern of administration that originates with lowest levels as in a bureaucracy, and in it, discretion of the top levels is reduced to near zero. The important characteristics of the administrative system progressively become the following:

(i) The people who know rules, and interpret them become central figures in the work life of the institution. The administrative personnel take on the critical role and by virtue of the nature of their work they become a power centre. As the rules increase in number, more staff is added to deal with "cases".

(ii) A hierarchy is needed to deal with

administrative problems. The processing of cases is done from lower to higher levels.

(iii) The discretionary elements in decision-making for senior and top management are reduced to the minimum. The institutional management is thus converted from an entrepreneurial to a bureaucratic structure. In this set-up decisions are based mainly on the rules and rarely on the judgement of the senior officers. It is often said by decision-makers that they fully see merit in a case but they cannot deviate from the rules and therefore are helpless to do anything in the matter. Deviation, if ever, invites criticism of playing favourites by the body of employees and often censor by audit agencies – both exert decisive influence on institutional practices. The employees criticise lack of dynamic leadership but many feel secure in a rule-hound system, especially the mediocre. The talented, in due course, become mediocre in their performance and choose to drift as do the less talented. Drift becomes an institutional characteristic.

(iv) The characteristics of work ethos as they develop over time are: Routinisation of work, lack of creativity, functioning through power group relationship to bypass the rules, alienation to work, lack of result orientation.

(v) The resulting pattern of leadership is often one of conformity, manipulation, liaison skills, fire-fighting and effective response to stress. The top and senior levels of management are constantly heard saying, "I work so hard but at the end of the day or a year I hardly know what I have achieved".

There are individuals who are able to isolate themselves from the prevailing work ethos and produce more than others. A large number of individuals however feel that they are able to create more during short visits abroad than they do in their home institutions. As mentioned earlier, the institutions operate through manipulative and power mould and employees react to these in several typical ways. The most common among these are the following:

(i) Isolation from the community.
(ii) Becoming a champion of the downtrodden or building power base by appearing to sympathise with those who suffer from feelings of victimisation.
(iii) Using the institution for personal ends either by ignoring institutional tasks, or by establishing links with power centres outside the institution, or by alienating from the institution or becoming hostile to it.
(iv) Assuming leadership in union-like organisations.
(v) Becoming submissive and a camp follower.

The dominant feeling of inadequacy, rejection, gratification of personal desires, fear of competition, fulfilling needs through manipulation and not achievement, dependency and the like are often imbedded in the unconscious mind. The cultural norms developed in the lower and upper middle class family, school and social environment are responsible for these patterns of behaviour. Many of these patterns are reflected in behaviour as adults. Employees find confirmation of these patterns in organisations. They are reinforced.

I will give some examples of the typical patterns of institutional behaviour as illustrations from my interviews:

* A top level trade union leader in one institution individually approached the chief executive to promote him. He said if the chief executive wanted to do this, he could. When pointed out that they themselves had strongly advocated a promotion policy and that decisions were taken according to the provisions of this policy, how should the chief executive now disregard the policy and take an independent decision in his case, the leader concerned kept repeating that the chief executive was a strong man and if he wanted to promote him, he could.
* A group of scientists who advocated an open and informal system, approached the chief executive in one institution to suggest that instead of guidelines, rules about training should be formulated. When asked if they disagreed with any of the decisions taken, the reply was that they did not. When pointed out that guidelines provide flexibility in evaluating individual needs, and therefore more beneficial to all concerned, while rules would have to spell out details of eligibility, cost, frequency, type, etc., and may deny many deserving cases the training opportunities, the reply was that people would know exactly what their entitlement was and, therefore, it should be specified. It was also pointed out to them, but to no effect, that this is how most institutions add one rule after another because the rules have to be modified to meet the requirements of many situations in an innovative institution. Most people see the semblance of security in a rule and this they need to satisfy their inner feelings of insecurity.
* One senior researcher assumed responsibility for several institutional tasks but turned suddenly hostile partly because he was not

considered suitable for a senior executive position. From that point he played the role of a champion of the downtrodden. He took aggressive postures in group meetings and blew up issues that would normally go unnoticed. The scientist concerned took up large projects, spent allocated funds but failed to prepare reports for any of these projects. Basically the individual concerned was afraid of success and found reasons to avoid responsibility.

* To provide varied experiences, a job enlargement programme was taken up by one institution. The section incharges were given responsibility for results. This task involved supervision of work of some class IV by Class III employees. Within a short time the concerned supervisors began to discriminate between one employee and another, threatened them with dire consequences and behaved with little understanding of the position. Within a short time greater control from higher authority had to be instituted to prevent serious industrial unrest.
* In a newly set up institution, departmental heads and employees kept referring to Government rules. When asked what was the logic of certain rules, the answer invariably was that the Government applied these rules. They neither questioned the logic of the rule, nor the need of a large numbers of the employees in the Government compared to their own. It was a case of blind acceptance of prevailing rules.
* In an established educational institution, the chief executive had limited telephone facilities. He was asked why was he not taking the decision to allocate telephones. His reply was that he had to wait for more lines because he

> could not give these to all members of the particular category of employees. When a suggestion was made that he could allot them on the basis of need or the best producers, his reply was that this would be unacceptable to the community of teachers. He said that criteria based on merit or need will be seen as discriminatory and cause social upheaval. On further testing the situation, I found that the chief executive was right and any criteria based on need or merit would not have been acceptable to the group. The chief executive of this institution was regarded as a very successful manager.

The need for standardisation, rigidity, rule-boundedness, etc., is felt, and promoted from within the institution, the same way as it is demanded by the promoter system. The need for standardisation by people in the promoter agency coupled with similar urges within the innovative institution provide an ideal setting for a rigid administrative arrangement for the institution. At both levels, however, there is constant need to bypass the rules so meticulously framed. A common saying in several organisations is that no one can manage efficiently without sidetracking some rules in some ways.

A social system that is maintained on a manipulative mould has difficulty in developing on open environment and, therefore, an effective collegiate or a consultative system. The existing patterns are likely to, and they in fact do, rest on suspicion, distrust and continuous manipulation. It is commonly believed by employees that rules are framed because of distrust in employees. I believe that the contrary is true. The rule-bound patterns of administration lead to what manifests in behaviour as suspicion and distrust; these patterns have system-base, and this phenomenon is rooted in the feeling of insecurity and a sense of dependency. The patterns will change if the members constituting the social system were able to recognise the dynamics of rule-boundedness and their dysfunctionality, or the child-rearing practices were to change which originate such feelings of insecurity and dependency among people. In the institutional context the first alternative holds true and ways have to be found to make the employees conscious of the phenomena.

Rigid and Bureaucratic

The overall impact of the Government's approach to standardise administrative practices of donor institutions is that the system tends to become rigid and bureaucratic. These features are further reinforced by standard audit procedures and interpretation of law courts that such bodies are the State.

It induces the administrative system to become more rule-bound than it would be if no pressures were exerted from exogenous sources. The Board is unable to exercise countervailing influence *vis-a-vis* the Government, and is unable to serve its intended purpose as all important issues relating to service matters, finances and programmes are essentially taken away from its purview. The Board may, at times, exercise influence through individuals but rarely as an entity.

Several factors together contribute to the ineffectiveness of the institutional management. No single factor accounts for the dysfunctionality of the management system. This analysis also suggests that improvement in the institutional management would have to include all the three areas simultaneously. This view is contrary to the general opinion among scientists that change in the role of the Government, and autonomy to the institutional management, would create suitable conditions in innovative institution for higher productivity. This is hardly probable. The employee culture and the role of the governance system are negative factors which contribute significantly to the in-effectiveness of institutions.

5

THE RATIONALE

The reasons for dysfunctionality in the behaviour of the contributory systems as discussed in the previous chapter must be understood from the dynamics and the compulsions of each system from within. The analysis of this dynamics must include the underlying assumptions about the people and the work organisation, and their perception of the innovative institutions. Any strategy to improve the existing system would have to examine the impact of these characteristics on the innovative institutions. Author will examine these compulsions in two ways, as follows: (i) Organisational compulsions and (ii) Social system compulsions.

The Organisational Compulsions

The dynamics of bureaucratisation of administrative organisations discussed here is not unique. Crozier (1964), Merton (1952, 1957), Mouzalis (1967) and others have discussed the phenomenon as also its consequences. Rules are made to bring order into the organisation, and induce a rational basis of decision-making. Rules are constantly modified or qualifications are added to incorporate features of a changing situation. Sections and sub-sections are added based on experience, precedence, or case law. In a rule-bound and rational-legal system, most employees adjust their behaviour and accept the rules as being absolute. They become central to their thinking. This may be one reason why most organisations in India have so many cases pending in administrative tribunals and courts of law.

McGregor (1960), Argyris (1964), Dayal (1967) and others have also discussed how assumptions underlying rules influence the behaviour of employees. If a manager believes that employees are shirking work, he would institute close supervisory practices. Employees might react to this and avoid work as soon as the supervisor turns his back on them. When the manager observes this behaviour he confirms his belief that employees are shirking work, and ignores the possibility that such behaviour may in fact be a reaction to close supervision and not an inherent characteristic of the employees. This is a self-fulfilling prophecy. The same employees in another institution may behave in a totally different way. Employees in a bureaucracy take rational-legal view and seek protection of the rules. Any deviation is unwelcomed.

Deriving from how Ministries in the Government perform their tasks, assumption underlying standardisation is that rules are independent of the task to be performed, and the rules do not influence behaviour. Hence rules can be universal, even if the behavioural pattern of the social organisation in any institution is different; the two can be dissociated. The findings of behaviour in organisations, however, do not support this contention.

While standardisation facilitates administrative controls, the intended arrangement rarely works. The decision-making in the Ministry is governed by considerations independent of the logic of the Board of Governors (BOG). In financial matters the Financial Adviser carries an unwritten veto over the Board. The prominent role of the Financial Adviser in decision-making is an extension of the pattern prevailing in the Government. This relationship is determined by factors such as the following:

(i) The Financial Adviser represents the Ministry of Finance in the concerned Ministry. He follows the directives of his "parent administrative Ministry", even if he is placed in an operating Ministry.

(ii) The Finance is seen to have a pervasive role in Government. In whatever terms the role of Finance is defined on paper, in public administration it plays the role of a super-agency. On paper it is feasible but only a few can in fact over-rule Finance. A cooperative Financial Adviser makes the job of the operating bureau easier; a difficult person can delay projects beyond reason. Both kinds are found in Government. The role of the Finance is also dependent on the interest that the administrative head of the Ministry, the Secretary, takes in the affairs of the institution, and the views he holds on various issues. Hence, the role of the Finance is a result of several interactive forces within the Department. The financial advisers take different views, and accordingly perform their role in different ways. As an organisational device for control and review, however, the Finance in public administration plays no significant role. The system is designed to control expenditure and little else.

The administrative bureaus have the accountability but there are repeated instances when the programmes are held up because financial "concurrence" for expenditure is awaited. The Finance can question manpower requirements, grades of staff, and almost every aspect of the project.

The super-agency role of Finance is seen to be inherent in the concept of public finance. All income is placed in the general fund and all units of the Government have to draw from this fund as per allocations. The Finance has to oversee the correctness and legitimacy of the expenditure. How this particular role is performed will partly depend on the individual concerned, but the questioning is legitimised in the system.

The concept of finance in better managed business organisations is different. The cost and profit centres are identified on a rational basis and financial data are used as an index of performance. This system provides relative autonomy to sub-units of the organisation. But this kind of autonomy is not built into pubic administration procedures.

Reforms brought about in the role of the Finance over the years have made little impact on the operating aspects of the Government. The quality of persons and personal relationships do make a substantial difference at work, but not the system.

(iii) The Ministry rarely feels responsible for the growth of an institution, especially at lower levels. Many officers give the impression that the Ministry grants a favour when it gives support to an institution. Often the degree of support depends upon a personal equation between the officials of the Ministry and the institutional management, and not on the sense of guardianship on behalf of the public by the Ministry concerned.

(iv) Most often the criteria employed by the Ministry for decision on requests from institutions is whether a particular practice exists in other institutions or not. It is assumed that all institutions are alike, and what is done for one should be done for all others.

(v) The support to an institution often depends on (i) how well does the administrative bureau get along with the Finance, and (ii) personal relationship that institutional managements are able to establish with the various functionaries in the Ministry and with the Finance. Hence, visits to all functionaries in the Ministry becomes a necessary condition of success. For this reason, among others, visits to the headquarters of the Government become an essential part of a chief executive's job.

A few typical examples will illustrate the points made here.

* When asked how he had been able to obtain more concessions from the Finance compared to other institutions, the chief executive of one institution explained his method of working as fallows:

  (i) He visits the Financial Adviser (F.A.) frequently and consults the officials in the Finance Division on all kinds of issues. Often he asks the officer concerned how best to prepare a case to get the concession. The officers feel important and have not failed to give what he asks for; (ii) Before the BOG meeting, the Chairman often has a discussion with the F.A. and seeks his advise on how best certain things can be done. Invariably solutions are suggested by the F.A.

* Many years ago, one chief executive went to the Finance Secretary to suggest that the institution can be revived only with devolution of technical and manpower resources; failing this, it would be advisable to close down the institution. The chief executive was asked to give a note on the subject. This was submitted. As usual the note was sent down to the "office". The contents of the note were known to everyone in the institution through the grapewine in "the office" and the rumour went round that the chief executive had recommended closure of the institution. While a great deal of misunderstanding resulted from this rumour within the institution, no response ever came from the Ministry. It was seen to be the chief executive's problem. The Ministry had no interest in its affairs.

The role of the Ministry *vis-a-vis* the Board is unclear. In many important areas concerning finance and service matters, the Ministry has veto power over the Board. Operationally the bind for Government nominees on the Board is severe. If the member has to represent the Ministry on the Board, he must have veto. If he has to be like any other member, he cannot be expected to bind the Ministry with the decision. If he does not represent the Ministry, it need not be an ex-officio appointment.

Assumptions underlying public administration are primarily rational-legal; it takes a highly mechanical view of the work system. It is assumed that personal feelings and relationship will not influence task performance. Rationality will govern executive behaviour. Each person will perform his task with care in an impersonal way. This perspective of a work organisation is simplistic. One consequence of this approach is that officers have to *use* the inherent power of their position in all activities with which they are associated. The authority of their official position is often extended to influence decisions in the semi-official and other institutional roles. In the meetings of advisory bodies, or institutions, the authority of the official position has to be often exercised to influence decisions.

The original idea that ex-officio nominees of the Ministry on the Board will enable the institution to obtain the required clearances from the Ministry more easily has not in fact been possible. The two roles are independent and operate as such. The officers concerned are not always able to link these roles. It is doubtful that they can do so. The priorities of the Government and those of any one institution need not be the same, except during periods of boom when each party can be given what they desire. The needs of institutions have increased and the competing demands and consequently pressures on the Ministry have multiplied manifold. Apart from competing demands and shortage of resources, many internal factors make decision-making extremely difficult. The most common among these are the specific directives of political leaders, the likes and dislike of officers, the desire to favour some and not others, and the need on the part of some to build up patronage. There are notable exceptions but no one senior enough in the Ministry has time to observe how it works.

The governance system is unable to shield the institution from standardisation. The terms of grant-in-aid, and the controls exercised through financial procedures of the Government, and directives, offer little scope for intervention. As discussed elsewhere, the Board may persuade or plead with the Government to accept certain views but there is no way that it can prevent standardisation. The nature of controls exercised by the Government, and the tendency to apply uniform practices in institutions must inevitably lead to centralisation.

How does the governance system work? The role of the BOG tends to become ritualistic. The Ministry has over-riding influence on the institution. If the dealing officers concerned in the Ministry have result orientation as individuals, the system works with reasonable understanding, provided the institution accepts their satellite role. If the dealing officers are power-oriented the system shows signs of strain. The system is designed for a high degree of control from the Government; some individuals specially at higher levels make controls less obvious. At times personal relationship make control less dysfunctional. The system works well or poorly depending upon the maturity of the individuals in the Government.

Social System Compulsions

As a detailed understanding of the social system is necessary, I have reported here the characteristics of four organisations, though the situation is typical of the innovative institutions. The institution has to deal with three segments of population:

(i) teachers and researchers (scientists).
(ii) professional staff such as library services, computer, relating to academic administration and engineering.
(iii) clerical and general services staff.

Each group has a different motive for joining the institution. The first group comes to the institution because they enjoy innovative work. An educational and research institution has no particular appeal for the second and the third group. Employees in the third group who value non-hierarchical and relatively less status-bound work environment develop preference for work in innovative institutions. Many other employees have no particular appeal for such institutions.

Traditionally most scientists consider themselves as a group apart and regard others as having a second-class status. The second group invariably compensate the feeling of lower social status in two ways. One, by being rigid in the interpretation of rules, procedures and the like to partially compensate for the lower social status and two, by going overboard to stretch the rules to accommodate exceptional requests of scientists. These persons who stretch rules derive vicarious satisfaction by accommodating scientists who have a higher social status and, by so doing, feel that they are their equal. The same people may not extend the same accommodation to the low-status groups and, by doing this, create resentment among employees. There are naturally a few who keep *normal* relations irrespective of social differentiation. The clerical employees generally attach themselves to scientists and obtain their protection. Some who are unable to find godfathers among the high-status groups feel left out from the mainstream of institutional activity. Invariably the activities are limited to educational and research work of the institution and support staff remain in the background. The more mature among the second and the third category of employees derive satisfaction by indirect association with achievements of the institution but many others react with hostility. In most innovative institutions the expression of this hostility is observed in several patterns of behaviour such as abusive language for scientists and the management, violent protests, shirking work and aggressive trade union activities. These patterns of behaviour are also caused and reinforced by many other practices, including poor behaviour on the part of some of the high-status groups. The hostility is, however, built-in in the structure of the institutional social system. Three typical examples would highlight the nature of the problems.

* When one chief executive pointed out to scientists that the tasks are interdependent and one group can hardly function without the help of other groups, the scientists found it difficult to accept that other groups can be given the same importance as themselves. They contended that they are engaged on the primary task and, therefore, they must be accorded central importance and all other employees should acknowledge their primary role. The view that the scientists will not be able to perform their tasks if they did not have the support services made little impression on them. Even the social scientists failed to recognise that social differentiation will generate inter-group hostility.
* Scientists often take it for granted that the support staff will do their bidding. There are many occasions when the staff members have considered the orders or behaviour of some scientists unacceptable and resented them. In many instances cases of non-obedience of orders have ended up as disciplinary cases, though mostly non-compliance is due to disrespectful behaviour of the superior and not the order *per se*. Not equality but lower status, and, therefore, compliance is taken for granted by the scientists.

In many educational and research institutions,

employees in category two and three have yet another serious problem. Most institutions have a limited number of positions at each level and a large number of employees have little scope for advancement. In a society where promotion and a high-sounding designation for a person is quite important and determine his social status, lack of promotional opportunity would lead to frustration and a feeling of helplessness. These feelings keep the situation for ever volatile. The employees or their unions take up many issues relating to service conditions but there is limited scope to find solutions to such matters. Confronting the institutional management either by the employees or the unions or covert protests such as suicide lead to inadequate solutions. The management can neither negotiate nor change service conditions, nor upgrade positions because these are subject to approval by the Government. The dissatisfaction tends to become a feature of the institutional life and both management and employees find themselves in what may appear as a hopeless bind. The institutions generally responds to it by accepting the drift. At times the institutional management changes certain service rules as ameliorative measures which, at times, create more serious problems in coming years. Examples of such decisions taken either wilfully or under pressure are innumerable. These are manipulative moulds and lead to instability of the social organisation.

In most cases employees have to either move out to secure higher level positions or they are given higher grades without change in the nature of their work. Not many employees want to leave their jobs, and only a few can get higher level positions. In some cases special grades are given to employees because they have no scope for promotion. These are artificial or contrived measures to deal with a situation. They offer no real solutions.

The only solution to the progression for employees lies in mechanising operations and employing a few numbers who can learn new skills on almost a continuing basis. The employees can improve their marketability and keep moving to different jobs within the institution or move out to better jobs. This strategy could apply to new institutions. The older and well-established institutions already have numbers far in excess of their needs. Even in such cases, progressive shift to higher skills and retraining may offer the only solution.

The Scientists

Author has discussed earlier that people in educational and research institutions have to have maturity and self-discipline, and that family and societal institutions develop contrary behavioural patterns. Among the scientists three patterns most often dominate. These are:

(i) Mature individuals who are greatly interested in their innovative work: they are highly task-oriented and cooperative. However, like many protected people, they are sensitive to criticism and get easily upset with rumours, gossip and hostile environment.

(ii) Highly self-centred persons who have little appreciation of, or interest in, the work of other people: some of these persons are often good producers. Their contribution is accepted by the peers outside the institution. They have, however, difficulty in getting along with other scientists within the institution and with support services personnel. Some self-centred persons have an exaggerated assessment of themselves and are not open to suggestions from others. They are invariably isolates, in the work community. Being self-centred such persons become activists in the community where their own interests are seen to be adversely affected. Normally they are marginal contributors to the life of the community.

(iii) Persons with limited capabilities, but over rate themselves as scientists. These persons are low producers, and seek compensation for low output in a variety of ways. They invariably become a focal point of discontent and champion the cause of the "downtrodden".

These are by no means pure categories. In each category there are many variations. Within the first two categories there are high as well as medium producers. Even the high producers keep wandering from one area of interest to another, and fail to realise their potential fully. Hence a system by which they can crystallise their interests and go deeper into some subject area is necessary.

In most institutions category three type of scientists create an environment of non-work. They respond poorly to pressures because the quality of their output is at best mediocre. They gain status in the social system by championing "causes" and in such efforts disturb the concentration of the other two categories. The quality of overall work environment will depend upon the mix of the above three categories of scientists and also upon the extent to which the second and the third category are successful in spreading discontent among the scientists.

The institutional management is generally unable to deal with the third category of scientists. Any precipitate action against them in Indian situation simply earns greater sympathy of other scientists. At the same time poor performance by these scientists sets a bad example to others and this matter is quoted by many in private discussions. Coupled with a poor system of rewarding good work, and discouragement to poor work, the result or output remains no longer a necessity for scientists, except for those who enjoy work for its own sake. The stage is thus set for the institution to drift and accept mediocre quality of output.

The category three type of employees are also found among other staff members. Such persons are also found in business organisations. Their negative influence in educational and research institutions is more pervasive than it is in business organisations. An important reason for this influence is that the nature of work in innovative institutions has to promote a relatively open and non-hierarchical system.

As mentioned earlier, these characteristics assume that individuals will develop self-discipline, and restraint and maturity. These features are not encouraged through child-rearing practices or social experience.

Early socialisation rewards dependence and opportunities are rarely given to develop a realistic assessment of personal abilities or self-appraisal. When people in such work environment are given freedom of expression and choice, some employees consider these as weakness on the part of the institutional management. Given the orientation for soft options among institutional managers, firm action is not taken to discourage unacceptable behaviour. Ignoring such behaviour encourages disrespect for stated norms of behaviour. Some employees interpret this leniency as weakness and allow the suppressed hostility to guide their behaviour. The hierarchical and role-bound relationships in a business or government organisation are however, an extension of the familiar system for employees.

Lack of Community Will

It is relatively easier for most employees to fall into a familiar pattern of role relationship in such organisations. The non-hierarchical relationships and relative degree of open relationships in an innovative institution being different, they satisfy some but, in many others, bring out suppressed anger and frustration. Adjustment to open a non-hierarchical system, and developing an identity and purpose in one's role, requires time and patience on the part of institutional management and the governance system. Another reason why deviants are not handled is the lack of Community Will.

The members of the community are unable to regulate the behaviour of deviant individuals. They do not take collective action. The community as a collective unit remains a spectator. The norm of behaviour is not enforced and partly because of this, the community fails to develop an identity (Whyte, 1969; Homans, 1950).

The deviant individuals gain positions of influence. It is left to management to perform the regulatory role. In such cases also, given the orientation of soft options and tolerance, the precipitate action by the administration invariably revives the feeling of personal insecurity. Thus the regulatory functions that the community must perform in a self-regulating and self-disciplining social organisation do not develop. Among the organisations studied many experiments to develop the community have been tried, each with varying degrees of success. Important as community function is in a democratic system, we would have to continue to experiment with new patterns as this kind of social environment is necessary for innovative institutions.

Areas of Development

A self-regulating social organisation makes heavy demands upon its members to regulate its affairs. Self-regulation will imply that norms of work and behaviour are generally accepted by the concerned people in the institution (the community) and each person will regulate his behaviour in accordance with the accepted norms. In case any member violates these norms, the community as a whole would regulate the behaviour of the deviant. Ideally a self-regulating community would have to develop a mechanism for determining norms of work and behaviour and ways of regulating behaviour of individuals.

In the institutions in the West the norms are generally accepted by the community and each member follows them within acceptable limits. Deviancy is handled on individual basis generally by the chief executive. Other members rarely interfere with executive action, or the right of the executive to take action so long as these are within acceptable limits.

In India norms are often set by the community. A large number of individuals, however, ignore the norms and the community is almost never able to regulate the behaviour of the deviant. The community is dominated or lead by employees in category 3 as described earlier, who champion the cause of the "downtrodden". Even those who disagree with such individuals seldom oppose them in public. As a result the whole community is constantly churned up for one reason or another.

The influence of the community as a collective unit is weak. Individuals choose soft options and wait for the executive to take action. Briefly, the social system has to gain maturity to establish, follow and regulate the community's behaviour. These social systems have to be developed in educational and research institutions. The demand on institutional leadership to develop such mature social systems is heavy. And a great deal of understanding and support on the part of the governance system would be needed to develop them. Considering the need for dependence, immediate gratification, self-centredness, power orientation, etc., the task of developing self-regulating social systems is by no means easy. Author believes, however, that internal systems will not be able to produce high quality output unless they were to develop a self-regulating system. Technical achievements and social regulation have both to develop together.

6

THE ACCUMULATED EXPERIENCE

The study of excellence in innovative organisations in a society which competes, and builds its superstructure on science, is a matter of natural concern for students of administration. Many studies have been reported in literature. I have summarised below a few trends from the published reports in the industrialised countries under two categories. These are:

(i) Nature of administrative system.
(ii) Sources of power and authority.

Nature of Administrative System

The administrative system is characterised by a great deal of self-direction and self-control. Selection of a scientist is done with care. The choice of a scientist is based on past record of work or potential. The scientist is given scope to "walk around" and see what line he would pursue within the overall direction of the particular laboratory or the institution. Recognised contribution is expected in five to seven years but generally the scientist talks to other persons, derives inspiration from "walking around" and sets his goals. Actual supervision of the work of the scientist is the minimum. Jackson (1985, p. 163) summarised the situation thus:

> "I have reviewed a number of aspects of the personalities of scientists and characteristics of productive environments. The implications are clear. Environments that nurture the creative urges of the scientist, that offer recognition for inventive productivity, that harness a concern for excellence, that communicate organisational goals effectively, that combine autonomy with accountability, that avoid imposing the burdens of rigid bureaucratic organisation and rules, that discourage non-scientist line administrators from close supervision of technical projects, and that offer monetary recognition and clear paths for scientists parallel to advancement have a reasonable prospect for success. Equally important, of course, is the careful selection of scientists and technical managers with a flair for the unique kind of leadership needed for scientific and technical development."

Setting high standards, helping the scientist to formulate a measurable goal, general supervision and creating what Harriet Zuckermann has called *evocative environment* is the essence of administration. Studies of Cavendish Laboratory, Bohr Institute, Laurence Radiation Laboratory and others show that scientists do better in certain groups and laboratories than in others. Commitment is inner-directed; the administrative environment strengthens it. A constant vigil, pinpricks through plethora of regulations and constant progress reports seem to distract scientists from their goals, and tend to become counter-productive. Arno Penzias, Vice-President of Research of Bell Laboratory (Bernstein, p. 231), says, "It is as much my personality as anything else. I demand a certain standard of myself and of everybody else".

Controls are implied in the relationship and not

through reports. Autonomy is highly valued by administration at Bell Laboratories. They have long-term perspectives both for individuals and the institution.

The literature also makes it clear that long-term expectations are quite specific. In case scientists do not achieve "usable" research in a specified period, say five to seven years, they are encouraged to leave or given administrative positions. Controls are personalised; so are rewards. There is no attempt at standardising the administrative system.

Scientists need interaction with those who can speak their language. Ideas develop and are cleared through such interaction. Secrecy does not encourage free interaction but openness does, and is encouraged in innovative organisations. Scientists also benefit by associating with professional associations and members to keep abreast of the frontiers of knowledge. In this respect support services such as library and library services, and overall progress reports are useful. In many laboratories, scientists make regular presentation of their research work and benefit from the critique by their peers.

In teaching establishments as well, collegiate culture and peer relationships play a crucial role in laying down the standard or the quality of work. At Yale University publication of one's research and consulting is encouraged as the critique of such publications ensures quality of output of the researcher.

The basic characteristics of innovative organisations in literature may be summarised as follows:

1. Institutions have a long-term perspective.
2. Scientists are encouraged and allowed considerable freedom to "walk around" and set

their long-term goals.
3. Supervision is personalised and in no sense directed at day-to-day work.
4. Commitment is seen as a complex phenomenon: the scientist has a high degree of professional involvement, pride of belonging to an institution with a reputation for high quality, and to his own work. The multiple areas of commitment are seen to be complementary and not competitive in effect.
5. The standards are set either by example or by peer group interaction and less by written rules.
6. Selection of scientists is made with great care and newcomers are allowed to judge suitability of the laboratory by arranging discussion with scientists, and visits prior to employment.
7. Strict control over budget and expenditure is maintained, as the scientist is given full freedom to choose and pursue his research. His worth is recognised by a suitably devised reward system.

Sources of Power and Authority

A scientist derives his authority from two sources: (1) his own contribution to knowledge, and (2) approval accorded to him from his peer group. It is achievement-based. He knows through prevailing norms that within a specified period he would have to show concrete results, and if he is unable to do so, it is unlikely that he can make a career in the institution. The approval is not politicised; on the contrary it is linked to achievement. This becomes his motivational power.

7

IMPROVING THE SYSTEM

Improvement of the system will require simultaneous action at two levels: (i) enabling changes at interface level, e.g. the perspective of the donor organisation and the governance system and (ii) the management of the institution including the social system and the managerial leadership.

The Government and the employee culture contribute significantly to the process of standardisation in innovative organisations. The Board of Governors (BOG) cannot serve as a countervailing force to moderate the impact of the two systems. The combined effect of these processes is that most educational and research institutions function much the same way as do Government offices. The bureaucratic orientation in administration condition the behaviour of scientists, resulting in a legal-rational perspective as against the innovative.

The concept of autonomy in Indian organisations is limited. It includes financial and administrative powers to individuals to carry out institutional tasks without undue delay. In many institutions even these powers are inadequate. The autonomy should also take into consideration the socio-political forces in the organisation. These forces determine the positioning of power centres in the organisation, the nature of the stresses and strains in the social relationships and contribute to the effectiveness or otherwise of the problem-solving and decision-making mechanisms within the organisation. The capability of the institutional management to effectively deal with the socio-political environment within the system will depend upon how well the governance system understands the nature of these forces, and the role that the Board members play individually and collectively. In some institutions the collusion between individual scientists and some members of the governance system has the effect of heightening the divisive forces, and in some others contact between the Board and the scientists has been remote. The institutional managers have to effectively deal with the socio-political environment, especially in the developing countries. The autonomy to institutional management should include both the freedom to handle socio-political issues as also work-related financial and administrative matters.

The improvement in the internal management of the institution cannot take place in isolation. It would require simultaneous action in those aspects that contribute directly to the ineffectiveness of institutional management. Hence the aspects that incapacitate the system would have to be handled as well as the aspects that facilitate the development of socio-technical system of the institution. One is unlikely to develop in absence of the other. These are not separable. The forces that critically lead to the ineffectiveness of the system are forces that lead to standardisation, inadequate level of autonomy and negative employee culture. The role of the governance system will have to change from passive to active and directional. The function of the Government in the entrepreneurial role, that of the Board of Governors in their directional role, and the employee culture in developing a socio-technical system are discussed in this chapter.

The Rationale

Ideally the Government in a democratic country such as India is an agency of the public to execute what is best for its well-being. In its role of *executor* the Government has to analyse what is good for the well-being of the society, at times with the help of committees of members drawn from the public, and also initiate ideas on its own and formulate programmes to achieve the desired goals. Within this context the Government has to perform a *promoter role*. It has to set up institutions that might contribute to the well-being of society, and provide such support as might be needed for the institution to serve its stated purpose. I have often heard some persons in Government and public organisations say that such institutions should earn their keep, at least partially. It has often been stated that management and technology institutions, for example, should support themselves. This view has been repeated many times and in many gatherings. Such institutions can become financially viable if they were to charge economic fees, or take up consulting projects, or receive donations from non-governmental sources. Alternatively they have to be attached to large business interests as the Bell Laboratories in the USA. In the event these institutions were to undertake sufficient amount of consulting and project work, the contribution towards research and teaching would have to be reduced as the kind of people who will come to a predominantly consulting organisation may be different from one that has predominantly teaching and research orientation. In many cases the main question remains: what contribution are these institutions created to make to public well-being?

The economic fees for such institutions is likely to be nearly 20 to 30 times more than the existing fees. Are these institutions created for those people who can afford the economic fee, or are they created also for upgrading the quality of education and research for a wide cross-section of the people and for the nation as a whole?

Donations for such institutions are unlikely to sustain even a part of their costs and it will be a long time before user organisations are able or willing to pay for education and research. The reasons for lack of such support are many. India has no trusts such as Nuffield, Ford, Rockefeller and the like. Trust laws do not encourage the creation of large trusts. Hence the relevant questions to ask are:

(i) Has the public need for such institutions been correctly assessed?
(ii) What mix of activities may generate partial funds for support without in any way compromising the quality of contribution expected of it?
(iii) How best to ensure that the institutional purpose is clear and specific and that it is being achieved?

The statement that institutions should support themselves has to be made with responsibility because public purpose that the institution is meant to serve should not be compromised. If the purpose if unimportant, public funds should not have been spent for creating the institution. The responsibility and decision to set up an educational and research institution is that of the Government and not of the institutional managers. At times approval for setting up some institutions is given for reasons other than public need. If such considerations have gone into the setting up of an institution, the responsibility for promoting and sustaining it must still be that of the Government. It is necessary to recognise that the responsibility for supporting an institution is an obligation that accompanies the decision to establish it, and this responsibility cannot be transferred to any other agency. This is the *basic position* that should govern relations between the Government and the individual institution concerned.

The Role of Government

Given this framework what should be the role of the Government *vis-a-vis* an institution. There are three possible roles that the Government could perform. These are:

(i) The entrepreneurial or promoter role having to do with setting down the particular contribution that an institution must make for public well-being. It includes initiating action and periodic review to determine how well the purpose is being served.
(ii) The Governance role having to do with the directional, goal-setting and exercising overall supervision to ensure that the managing system is operating in a way that is both efficient and effective. This is generally a collective role of the Board of Governors of the institution.
(iii) The managerial role having to do with influencing administrative action for managing the institution.

The first two roles are essential for the Government as the guardians of public interest. The third role as now performed leads to a high degree of standardisation and in limiting autonomy of the institution. These terms are used as they are defined earlier and, in this sense, create dysfunctionality in the system.

Even in the performance of the first two roles, the government system poses serious problems. Individual officers find it difficult to effectively respond to the institution's requirements even when they want to do so. The major areas of handicap are identified below.

Project Approval System

The system of planning is casual and rarely leads to commitment on the part of constituent members of the Government. When a project is conceived, it has to be approved by an inter-ministry group. The purpose of this exercise is to satisfy that the project is worthy of support and, if approved, the Government as a whole will undertake to support it. Assuming that the project has to be financially supported, and the duration of the project including its gestation period is five years, the funding is done for one year at a time. This is done because Government budgets are approved on an annual basis while the project needs support for the entire period of five years. If the income of the Government is reduced in the following year, or on unexpected level of expenditure becomes necessary due to unforeseen causes like famines, floods and the like, the funds for the institution are cut, sometimes drastically. This has happened with several projects.

The approving procedure worked reasonably well when the number of projects was small and the foundation grant, though difficult, could somehow be managed. Many of the projects had public people who had a promotional interest in it. Such persons were able to influence decisions in the various Ministries of the Government. The persons like Kasturbhai Lalbhai, S.S. Bhatnagar, Homi Bhabha, Vikram Sarabhai and others were such mediators. The proliferation of projects and lack of mediatory influence in the present context make the system unsympathetic.

Under the circumstances the first area of improvement is planning and the method of committing Government resources to projects. The nature of improvement needed in this respect is discussed below:

(i) The project financing should be treated differently from the maintenance or what is called non-Plan budgeting. The project funds must be planned for a two-to three years period if not for the entire project. On paper this system is generally accepted but in fact this situation does not prevail. A detailed history of projects would show the reality.

(ii) It is assumed that all necessary care is exercised when inter-ministerial approval is given for the project. In effect, the senior people are unable to give sufficient time to examine the project. At times projects are approved without full appreciation of the implied commitment to support it. Some projects are approved because none is willing to question its relevance, or approval is given on consideration of friendship, mutual exchange of favours among the officers in the Ministry, implied political pressure and the like. The laid-down procedure implies commitment of the Government as a whole, but it turns out that the responsibility is relegated to the Ministry concerned. Often the Ministry is unable to support the project at the scale necessary due to budget cuts. The system amounts to saying, "We may have approved the project because you wanted it, now you do the best that you can – we wish we could be sympathetic to you but you will have to wait for good time to come". The entire process of appraisal of the project and its approval has become a mechanical exercise, and given the tendency for soft options in the Indian environment, no hard reality is faced. The implications of such approval are rarely felt and responsibility for joint approval is hardly accepted.

(iii) The lack of joint responsibility may have somewhat less serious consequences if the responsibility within the Ministry for the project was accepted by all concerned. The project is seen to be that of the division concerned and not that of the Ministry as a whole. Hence prioritisation of projects and fund allocation go through an extremely complicated process. In this tussle the project often becomes an orphan.

Every large organisation has to operate at least at three levels: (i) the level of a department, a bureau in the Government (ii) the autonomous sub-unit such as a field office or a Ministry, and (iii) the organisation as a whole, the Government. As such the Government would have to recognise the distinction between operations or decisions at each of these levels. This distinction is necessary to recognise the degree of commitment on the part of the Bureau, the Ministry, and the Government as a whole. If participation in decision-making does not lead to commitment, little purpose is served by referring projects to intra-Ministry or inter-Ministry committees. The Ministry bodies involved in the projects, and a positive decision to support it should be taken as a commitment to it. The decision should not be a casual affair. Officers who form membership of such committees are overwhelmed with papers and files and are rarely able to examine issues in depth. Most matters travel up to the top-level personnel. Given this circumstance, the individuals concerned have neither the time to study the project nor to understand its particular features nor even the purpose fully. If decisions are taken in a casual way and fresh points are made later when the project is already in operation, such approvals would have little purpose. The data shows that initial scrutiny of projects is generally weak and approval is seen to be a formality and not a commitment. Seldom if ever a decision taken at intra- or inter-ministry level is final. Fresh questions are always raised at every stage of the project.

Ex-officio Board Membership

Officials from the Ministry are made ex-officio members of the Board to provide a link between the Ministry and the institution. The purpose was to smoothen through this link the process of clearing sanctions or approvals by the Government with full awareness of the Board's views. But this purpose is not served.

The reason being that the officer is placed in a bind. He can operate in one of the following two possible ways:

(i) The dynamics of decision-making of the Ministry is complex. It has its own pulls and pressures, as well as a rationality. The decisions are based on many factors such as priorities defined by the Government or the Ministry, the power and prestige of the individual exercising the pull, the rationality of the situation, the Ministry's assessment of the need of the institution and likes and dislikes of the persons requesting assistance or those examining such issues in the Ministry. If decisions were based on mutual understanding between the institutional managers and the Ministry, and rationality, the demands would be realistic. The approach will be how to jointly solve problems rather one of giver or taker.

(ii) Within the Ministry the allocation of funds depends on competing considerations such as the perceived importance of the programmes, the prestige of the sponsor of a particular programme, the administrative bureau and the finance. Given this complex decision-making situation, and an almost unlimited demand by public bodies for support, the Ministry's nominee invariably cannot commit himself to a decision in a Board meeting. He can only say that he will examine the matter. At times he has to yield to departmental compulsions even when he, as an individual, is sympathetic to a proposal. To cope with the awkwardness of the situation, a convention has developed by which discussions on matters of finance and service matters are first held in the Ministry and these decisions are ratified by the Board. The implication of this arrangement is that the Board which has responsibility for the institution has no real say in important matters concerning budget, funding and service matters. Even on other matters that have financial implications, the Ministry concerned has a decisive role. Invariably these matters are handled in one of the following ways:

(i) The Board members exercise their collective pressure to persuade the ex-officio members to agree to the proposal.

(ii) The Board requests the Financial Adviser

to examine the matter and give his recommendation to the Board, which becomes a decision in most cases.

(iii) The Board in rare cases requests the Chairman or a Committee to write to the Ministry, or meet the Secretary or the Minister to have the matter examined.

The role of the nominee of the Ministry is rather awkward. Often such members qualify their statement by saying that they are speaking in their private capacity. At times they are put under undue pressure to agree to a proposal. In either case the role of such members is ambiguous. If they represent the Ministry as an official, they must have matters processed in the Ministry before the meeting. This is why most nominee members come with written comments prepared by their office staff on each item of the agenda. But this processing is not as complete as it is when the matters are referred to the Ministry for decision. Yet, the member concerned is placed in the situation where he must commit the Ministry. The nominee members would have to have a veto if the Board disagrees with him. In case he does not have a veto in practice, he will be hard pressed to carry on the work in the Ministry. On the other hand if he has the veto, all other members have little to contribute to the *direction* of the institution. We have created an awkward situation both for the nominee members and the Board. In practice, however, Board members allow such matters to be decided by the Ministry and avoid confrontation. This is because most members recognise that confrontation will serve little purpose. As the autonomy of the Board is greatly curtailed, the members feel less involved in the affairs of the institution than required of their role. The governance system thus tends to become a formal institution and is placed poorly to perform its assigned role.

In the West it is rare that any donor institution is involved in managerial decisions. The chief executive and his team has the autonomy to manage the affairs of the institution in the best possible way to achieve its purpose. It is also rare that interlocking roles are created in institutions which have built-in potential for conflict. It is also rare that any one person has the veto power over the views of many.

The Financial Rules

The financial rules of the Government applicable to the Ministries and departments are extended to the autonomous units. The provisions prescribe the procedures for approval, audit, budget review and the like. Once prescribed procedures are applied, the institution becomes like other departments and remains no longer autonomous.

It is unlikely that institutions can be freed of unnecessary restrictions without the financial autonomy. Change in the financing of the institutions is necessary to transfer responsibility for governance to the Board.

Because of the pattern of funding, the institution can only make plans annually. The funds approved are given subject to approval of Parliament. The grant-in-aid is reduced on an ad hoc basis without knowledge of the institution.

The first instalment of the grant often reaches the institution about three months after the financial year begins. Thus (i) the availability of funds is erratic, and (ii) use of funds is to be made in a period of nine months. The long-term planning of institutional activity and programmes is, therefore, difficult.

The three main disadvantages of Government funding of institutions are:

(i) All the directives applicable to normal administrative Ministries of the Government apply automatically to the funded institutions. The audit, the purchase, the financial practices which may be relevant for a vast organisation of the Government are generally irrelevant and wasteful for smaller organisations.

(ii) The institutions fall under the court's interpretation of a State and these institutions are expected to follow the practices applicable to Government employees. This requirement contributes to standardisation, as discussed earlier.

(iii) The institutional management become dependent on the Government for funds. When they are short of money they look to the Government to bail them out, and not examine alternative sources or activities for generating resources. The institutional management succeed on account of their liaison skills and not performance. While public support for innovative work is essential because these activities are not likely to be self-financing, the institutional management should share the responsibility for growth.

The financial autonomy is needed for autonomous institutions to become more self-contained and responsible for results. This kind of autonomy will be possible only if a trust fund were to be created which can give fixed income to the institution. The trust fund is a device to provide independence and security to the institution, as also place upon them the responsibility for growth. The expenses beyond the normal levels should be obtained by the institutional management through research and project funding sources. The normal 10 per cent or so increases in expenses would have to come from trust income but the institution should assume responsibility for additional requirements through internal efforts. The trust fund could be increased by donations, or surplus from income.

The trust funds could always be invested in development programmes and the Government will not have to take away large sums of money for this purpose. Such a scheme has generally not been acceptable to the Government. Perhaps the reason is the fear that the Government will lose control over the institutional management. This argument appeals more to those officers who are power-oriented; some others fear that in our system whatever little contribution to the national purpose these institutions make will be lost and the institutions will drift. The governance system is not strong enough to deal firmly with the non-performing institutional management. I hold the view that there is need to make the governance system stronger than to perpetuate dependence of institutions -- a circumstance that contributes to their ineffectiveness.

It is true that most institutions in India have partially or mainly failed to serve the purpose for which they were created. The reason for this performance may, at least partially, lie in the handicaps under which these institutions function. Poor achievement is a universal feature of all organisations in Indian situation. This assessment applies equally to in organisations such as the public service, the business, the Government. We have to identify how improvements in each of the organisations can make them less constrictive for the growth of others. We should not confuse cause and effect for poor performance.

In brief three areas of improvement in the Government-institution relations are necessary. These are:

(i) The procedure for approval of projects by the Government should carry greater seriousness than it does. Approval of a project by intra- and inter-Ministry committees should imply commitment to the project. Such an approval by an inter-Ministry Committee should imply the Government's commitment to a successful completion of the project, and joint effort to ensure planned level of support to it. In most cases the people sitting in these committees have not even studied the project fully and the decisions are taken in a casual manner. Questions about the project are raised much after the project goes on stream.

(ii) The Government's role as an owner of the project is at times not fully reflected in its relations with the project management. Some officers deal with the project as if they are obliging the institutional management or by agreeing to a proposal, they are bestowing a favour upon them. The Government is the owner of the project in its role as guardian of public interest. The success or failure of the project, as owner, becomes the Government's responsibility. The concept of Government responsibility for the success of the project is poorly understood at lower levels of the hierarchy and few senior persons in the Government have time to inculcate this perspective.

(iii) The autonomy for institutions will be possible only if they have financial independence. The Government has been reluctant to consider giving educational and research institutions financial autonomy although the intention is categorical in the Education Policy of 1987. One feasible solution is to create a separate trust for some of the institutions of higher learning. The trust funds can be invested in national projects to reduce additional burden on the Government. This or another proposition that can give financial autonomy to educational and research institutions is necessary and we need to experiment with new patterns of financing institutions.

The Governance System

No single person should have absolute powers. Autonomy is necessary to perform the task, and appropriate administrative systems have to be evolved to achieve results. It is necessary for a knowledgeable group of public men to be closely associated with the direction and review of the institutional tasks. Such a body is the Board of Governors. It has been my good fortune to serve on several Boards where members take keen interest in the affairs but meetings tend to become casual because all important matters are decided outside the Board. The Board of Governors rarely perform the tasks fully that are laid down in the charter.

The BOG has also to be aware of the sensibilities of a socio-technical system that has need for a collegiate pattern. The management must develop self-regulation. They alone can set standards of quality and take the necessary remedial measures. The task system also requires that they contribute towards goal setting and direction for the institution. The BOG has to lay down parameters within which collegiate-level tasks can be performed. Often implications of the collegiate system and boundary conditions that separate the BOG and the management are not articulated. As a result the Boards on which I have served hardly contribute anything significant to the institution. They either deal with trivialities which are beyond the defined financial and administrative powers of the Director, or take over matters which scientists can perform better than the BOG.

In educational and research institutions, controls are different from the administrative organisations. Such institutions have to develop a complex planning system for institutional activities. The Board would have to provide overall direction, leaving detailed planning to the scientists. The institutional management would have to integrate the plans and determine how best the institutional purpose can be achieved.

The Board's primary functions would consist of seven aspects:

(i) Boundary control function protecting the institutional management from outside forces that would interfere with the normal work of the institution. If there is public criticism or uniformed critique of the institution, the BOG should satisfy themselves about the situation and, having done so, either take action to correct the situation or protect those who are victimised.

(ii) Ensure that the management and the members are motivated enough to give their best to the institution.

(iii) Determine overall directions for institutional activities, review plans and judge broadly if the quality of work is satisfactory.

(iv) Ensure that resources needed for institutional activities are adequate and, if not, provide the support needed to set the situation right.

(v) Ensure that long-term plans are prepared and

are satisfactory, keeping in view the purpose for which the institution is set up.

(vi) Dealing with appeals against the decisions of the chief executive.

(vii) Appointment of key personnel of the institution.

The Managing System

Innovative organisations have unique task features compared to business or administrative organisations. Each scientist is a specialist in his own area of study. The hierarchy neither represents capability, nor experience. The power is ideally gained by members through intellectual contribution and less through experience. Basically each scientist is engaged in a unique task yet there must be facility to learn from others, and an environment that generates the urge to learn. The system has to be flexible and open. These characteristics and others like it have to be developed an harboured by the management of an innovative organisation.

To identify the characteristics of the internal management system, I will examine the framework comprising the five characteristics that author had taken up for analysis in Chapter 2, and discuss what successful institutions have done in this respect. The five characteristics are:

(i) The socio-technical system
(ii) The concept of autonomy
(iii) The concept of standardisation
(iv) The concept of power or politicisation
(v) The concept of equilibrium or balance

(i) *The Socio-technical System*

The institution has to provide considerable flexibility

to scientists in their work. Flexibility is needed in the choice of a project by interacting freely and purposefully with others. One teaching institution in a professional area allowed a newcomer to move around freely for six months to collect teaching material from the field, to absorb through interaction the teaching philosophy and become familiar with new educational approaches. The careful process of socialisation helped this institution maintain a high quality of teaching. The institution offered opportunity to learn but the indirect and subtle learning environment in this situation was provided by peer levels.

Interaction among scientists with different backgrounds is necessary. Some institutions provide this facility by not having a rigid departmental structure, or by promoting sentient system which brings together scientists who share a common interest and a common language. Other institutions provide more structured activity around seminars, research presentations, workshops and other such activities as offer free interaction in the work community. Assuming that the primary motive of a scientist to pursue his profession is to enhance learning, the social system must provide scope for increasing the knowledge of his universe.

Successful institutions have clarity about their mission and have long-term plans to serve the purpose. Research institutions with emphasis on pure research need different social organisation than institutions that have bias for applied research. It is found that greater interaction between scientists and user organisations is necessary for applied research. In most cases a link position between the two improves the output of both. The link position must understand the language of both the scientist and the user.

Innovative institutions promote long-term goals

which are specific. The successful institutions have result orientation and they take action in case the results do not come. The Vice-President of Research at Bell Laboratories, Amo Penzias, himself a Nobel Prize winner, says about their philosophy (Bernstein, 1988, p. 232):

> "One of the things that people are constantly amazed at in this place is just how little short-term management there really is, just how little short-term management I get. People don't believe that nobody tells me what to do on a daily, weekly, or even a monthly basis. Occasionally I get a little bit of 'fatherly' advice, but in the past year I do not think I have spent as much as four hours with my boss, discussing how I should be doing my job. Instead we focus on our long-range objectives."

Earlier, Penzias says, "But we also have to understand, and I think our owners do, that it can take years and years before someone may be able to make something useful out of a piece of pure research".

Some of the best research institutions take scientists away from research if they show unsatisfactory results over time and place them in administrative positions or send them away. Poor output is not accepted. This norm will be hard to establish unless high-quality output was expected and it were to become a norm of work place.

(ii) *The Concept of Autonomy*

Soldiers sent to the battlefield with one hand tied behind them rarely win battles. This may seem to be more an Indian bureaucratic phenomenon than a universal one. A Chief Executive could not be waiting for instructions of the Board on matters of day-to-day administration. He must have authority to deal with matters that contribute to the health of the institution.

Successful institutions use two kinds of control. The most common is based on results. The second is based on peer review of performance. Some teaching institutions encourage scientists to prepare a work plan and review their achievements against the plan. Seminars based on work done are used to review the progress and control quality.

Controls are personalised and are non-bureaucratic in nature. They facilitate progress, and rarely consist of just filling up standard progress reports.

The second feature of controls is that peer groups set standards of quality and output. They are not seen to be imposed upon individuals by the "management", or a body external to the institution. The skill of the management lies in developing autonomous groups which are able to regulate their own affairs.

(iii) *The Concept of Standardisation*

In most effective institutions, rules are kept to the minimum. They are framed by the management to suit the particular circumstances. The reward and punishment is an inherent feature of the rules of the institution. As discussed earlier, reward and punishment in most Government-supported institutions does not operate due to the rigidity with which rules are framed and operated.

The Abid Hussain Review Committee of the CSIR in its Report (p. 4) comments:

> ". . . the culture of work in the CSIR, as in many other institutions in our society, has two distinct

> attributes. There is little reward for performance and there is no penalty for non-performance. There is, hence, an accumulation of scientists past their prime which is reflected in the rising age composition and the near absence of mobility. These problems are compounded by the fact that the CSIR functions like a department of the Government rather than as a society. This has tended to foster hierarchy or bureaucracy and stifle creativity. It is ironic that the culture of the Government has become dominant while the culture of science has become subordinate in the CSIR."

In formulating rules, assumptions made about the behaviour of employees is important. One organisation which has now grown large in numbers started with the assumption that employees are responsible and they will purposefully regulate their behaviour, given freedom. This organisation has no leave rules, or leave application forms or a laid-down procedure. Employees tell their superior officer when they have to be away and adjust their needs in such a way that immediate work does not suffer. The average number of days of leave taken by employees in this organisation is lower than in most comparable organisations. The behaviour is regulated by individuals themselves, and not their supervisors. This organisation has totally different personnel practices than other comparable organisations. People are influenced by the intention underlying the rules, even if it is not explicitly stated in them. While no social system can work without rules, the management of successful institutions develop an appropriate mix of rules, conventions and norms that guide behaviour and relationships in an institution. A particularly difficult problem in setting conventions and norms as against rules in the Indian context is the felt need for structure on the part of employees who feel secure with rules than with conventions. One institution tried to develop a representative council of all employees to develop norms for the behaviour of the community but pulls for bipartite relations prevented this multi-level representative body from effectively functioning. The council had to take up self-review exercises but as a body they failed to serve this purpose. Self-awareness is necessary to develop a social system that is in harmony with task requirement, and institutions would have to create environment best suited to their purpose. This effort will be difficult if urge for standardisation on the part of the donor body is as comprehensive as discussed earlier.

(iv) *The Concept of Power or Politicisation*

Power and politics are an inherent part of an organisation. Internal institutional processes create groups and inter-group pressures. The groups who feel deprived, or less favoured, develop hostile feelings towards groups that are seen to occupy privileged positions. Some groups think differently from others and want to impose their will on the work community as a whole. Groups in an organisation are ubiquitous. Different groups exercise influence over others in the community. The individuals and groups play games with one another. These processes constitute the core of politics in the organisation. The institutional management has to manage these political games. Each organisation develops its own political behaviour and the styles would vary from one institution to another.

Another kind of politicisation in institutions is when outside organisations or people influence the decision-making, or work. This aspect of politicisation causes dysfunctionality as local needs of the particular institutions become subordinate to the needs of another person or another organisation. When this phenomenon occurs, the harmony and internal consistency of administration is lost.

In the Indian context the second kind of politicisation is also common. The only two ways the influence of the external bodies is prevented from the disruptive features are, first, when the Board of Governors are able to take full command of institutional affairs, and secondly, the institution has internal strength to withstand such influences. It is unlikely that politicisation can be prevented except where these two conditions prevail.

(v) *The Concept of Equilibrium or Balance*

The institutional management has to achieve a balance between several kinds of opposing force: the donor groups and the scientists, the staff and the scientists, different levels of staff with varying needs, the Board and the varying needs of the staff, and many such groups. The most powerful among these and the ones that influence the administrative system of the institution are three: (i) the donor agency, (ii) the Board of Governors and (iii) the different levels of employees.

Of the three, the Board should exercise the most influence. But, in the Indian context, the Board, in most cases, exercises the least influence. The decisive influence is the donor agency and the employees. It is, however, necessary that all three understand their role in the process of developing an institution because without serious effort in this direction, it is unlikely that institutional management can perform its role effectively.

Leadership for an institution is necessary but its

effectiveness is reduced if the stacks piled against it weigh heavy. In such an event the attention of the leader is primarily diverted to maintenance of the social system than developing it. The effectiveness of the leadership and the productivity of the innovative institution are likely to be indifferent, if changes are not comprehensive relating to the system as a whole.

The experience of successful innovative institutions abroad shows that leaders best suited to lead such institutions must have appreciation of the requirements of research as a task and that of the scientists. Leaders who have experience of administrative organisations may generally have difficulty in appreciating the sensibility of an innovative situation and the people in it. It is unlikely that institutions can attract sufficient people to shoulder the responsibility unless the system was less demanding and offered scope for creative administrative leadership.

8

SOME GENERALISATIONS

A discussion of innovative institutions provides material for postulating certain propositions about the health of organisations especially in the environment of developing societies. These postulates relate to two aspects of work organisations:

1. Organisational Analysis
2. Social Organisation

Organisational Analysis

Four kinds of consideration are necessary in analysing organisations. These are:

(i) Systemic considerations;
(ii) Administrative factors;
(iii) Organisational factors; and
(iv) Institutional leadership.

(i) *Systemic Considerations*

The first proposition is that innovative organisations would have to accept democracy as a way of life. This pattern of life is necessary due to two overwhelming factors: First, the need to adjust to changes in the environment and the expectations of new people entering the job market; and second, the pressures of competition and new technology tend to make higher demands on the innovative abilities of individuals and groups. And of the known social patterns democracy is able to generate these more than any other kind of social organisation.

The expectations of younger people entering the job market are guided by the relative liberalisation of education, increasing awareness of citizen rights generated by the spread of such values in political declarations, through the mass media, specially the TV and the cinema, and caste or work group organisations such as trade unions, religious bodies and the like (Dayal, 1990). Organisations which relied on family-like and paternal relationships report that the younger people feel that their eligibility to organisational resources should be determined as a matter of right and not as a favour bestowed upon them by management. Employees in an organisation, which had no leave rules and leave could be taken according to one's needs, feel that they would much rather know what is their right than depend on someone to grant them leave. This kind of consciousness about rights is sharper among the younger generation than it was among the earlier generations. If these changes are not recognised by organisational management and reflected in administrative practices, it is likely that these people would grow hostile to the organisation and militate against the established order. The need for self-expression at work will grow and personnel practices would have to take notice of changes in the expectations of employees, if only to avoid militancy. These considerations would apply equally to organisational management as also the large organised bodies such as the trade unions.

The studies of high-tech industry, automated manufacturing and office administration show that certain decisions would have to be taken as close to the operating positions as possible (Dayal, 1988; Child, 1984). The newer technology is changing the role of the operative. Greater awareness, knowledge and involvement is necessary at lower levels of the operating positions. This factor would have a profound influence on work organisation.

A related proposition is that democratic systems function well by self-regulating and countervailing organisms that influence the social organisation. This aspect needs explanation.

Countervailing System: Democratic society has to encourage self-regulating groups or countervailing forces that are capable of achieving a balance between organisms that exercise pulls in opposite directions. The labour union strength has to match the strength of the management, the consumer organisations have to balance poor quality manufacture, the student bodies have to balance poor quality teaching, and so on. These forces or organisms achieve a state of equilibrium and enable the various elements of society to regulate themselves. They determine the norms that should govern various organisms. If any of the countervailing systems are weak, the opposite force would create a social imbalance. The weaker force will try to compensate its weakness by becoming hostile to the opposing force, or show its weakness in a variety of other ways such as corruption, passivity and the like. At times the Government as a public agency has to step in to bolster the weaker system. In such an event the intervening agency (the Government) has to judge the measures, the manner and the period for extending a supporting hand, because the purpose of such support is to make the weaker sub-system strong enough to perform its social purpose or the countervailing role. The science of public policy is mainly concerned with such issues.

In a developing society there are many social imbalances because many countervailing organisms or groups in the community are weak. The unions are generally unstable and need support. The consumer force is almost absent. Students on their own make little contribution toward improvement of teaching. None of these are able to perform a countervailing role. Many such groups need support for full maturation, and generally the Government provides this support. However the difference between a democratic and a totalitarian society is that in the former the nature of support is meant for strengthening the countervailing institutions in order that the community can regulate itself, and in the latter the Government controls these institutions to regulate them so that it can control the community think.

Within an organisation a democratic social system would have to develop countervailing sub-systems so that the community or society can, by and large, regulate itself. The community has to evolve a value base that is generally acceptable to most members. The Board of Governors have to be constituted from among carefully chosen public men who can exercise *wise* choices in overseeing the affairs of the institution. Any impulsive action of the chief executive has to be moderated by the BOG and Academic Councils. The teacher autonomy must be moderated by student representative bodies, and by committees which involve employees. When all these bodies work with optimum effectiveness, and perform their social countervailing roles, the social system encourages a balanced growth. It is true that developing a democratic basis for a society is difficult; yet it is essential for a democratic social order to prevail. In order to move in the direction of establishing a democratic social system, the first requirement is that we are clear of the concept, and then the notions of how best to operationalise it.

It is, at times, stated in literature that democratic functioning inhibits innovation. This is a misconception. Innovative ideas develop when autonomy is given and observed, in a role, not by disregarding role-boundary of other roles. Creativity is enhanced when each group tries to improve its own effectiveness and, by this action, edges others to improve their effectiveness. An organisation achieves optimum results when all sub-systems improve and not by achieving excellence in parts.

In innovative institutions, individuals primarily determine the role boundary and, therefore, the concept of self-sustaining social system is important for creativity and health of such institutions. If a single person or a group, except for specific reasons and for a limited period, carries unlimited power in an organisation, such an institution in a democratic or open society is likely to weaken itself in the long run. This proposition is especially relevant for institutions that rely primarily on individuals for institutional tasks. Educational and research institutions fall in this category. They will not be able to institutionalise innovation, if they become dependent on one man's or one group's innovative efforts. When this person leaves or the group weakens, the institution will experience a vacuum. Traditional business organisations are hierarchical and could possibly function with top-down directives; the same strategy is likely to be ill-suited for research and educational institutions.

The consultative decision-making structures in educational and research institutions is a necessity. However, directional review and appraisal of a public institution must rest with the public for whose benefit the institution is created. Such a body must be the Board of Governors who represent public interest, assuming that they are carefully constituted to serve this purpose. The ultimate power must lie with this collectivity. The Board as a collectivity is a countervailing system to institutional management. A compromise of the functioning of this collectivity is likely to disturb the balance of the countervailing system in the institution. In India the role of the Government in operating terms is absolute and creates an imbalance in terms of both the governance system and the institutional management and, in turn, weakens the institution.

(ii) *Administrative Factors*

The influence of rules and regulations on the administrative system is inadequately recognised. Simon refers to the administrative system as one that insures action, or achievement of results. It includes the mechanism for goal-setting, achieving wider acceptance of goals, integrating individual and corporate goals, and motivating individuals and groups to achieve planned results.

The top management's view of man and of work also influences the nature of administrative system (Dayal, 1970; McGregor, 1960). The top management who believe in developing men promote more open consultative system, and persons with contrary beliefs surround themselves with rigid patterns. Those who believe that people should derive pleasure from work are concerned about various forms of work organisations; others may assume that bureaucratic structures apply universally.

The educational and research institutions require open, less formal systems in which individuals consider it normal to interact. The open system management would have a greater degree of meaningful interaction both at peer and hierarchical levels. These relationships would depend on trust that subordinates have in their supervisors. The goal-setting and review methods would invariably require participating systems, needing a variety of consultative structures for decision-making.

Administering rewards and punishments in Indian organisations pose many problems, even at the top of the pyramid. In educational and research institutions any deviation from the established pattern is resented. Reasons for resenting merit reward for good work and punishment for poor work are many.

Most employees fear that personal likes and dislikes or favouritism might overshadow performance. This is true in a number of organisations. Another reason for this practice is the sense of personal inadequacy that many individuals feel in their jobs. This feeling is sharper when some are given recognition and others are left out (Dayal, 1976). The sense of insecurity comes from highly protective child-rearing practices (Chattopadhyay 1987; Dayal, 1979). The personal inadequacy is as significant as the organisational malpractices. The corrective measures for organisational issues are easier to handle than the personal feelings of inadequacy. The people have to recognise the feelings, would have to have the desire to correct it and have the psychological strength to work on it.

Punishment arouses fears of victimisation. People at higher levels are seen as father figures. Any perceived threat to isolate people whose performance is poor raises fears of rejection, due mainly to overly protective childhood experiences. The administration will have to deal with emotional insecurity and dependency as with objective appraisal systems for rewarding good and discouraging poor performance.

The other administrative factors of direct concern are: (a) size of institution and (b) the nature of control systems.

Size of Institution: In the Indian context it is necessary to recognise that the social and task systems are intertwined. Few people are able to draw a distinction between social and work roles. People would have to learn the distinction between the two. The size of the organisation should be such as to enable a nurturent system to develop. The size should be increased only when the social system settles down. If this phase of settling down is not evaluated with care, the total system could suffer from turbulence for indefinite periods of time.

Nature of Control Systems: In educational and research institutions the controls are generally inadequate. Attempts have been made to use concepts from business organisations to institute systems of control in innovative institutions. These are not always appropriate or sufficient. The main activity being education and research, measures to improve the quality of these activities are important, especially in India where market feedback data are often unreliable. The product being in short supply, the market response or demand is not a good enough index of quality.

The controls relating to the administrative aspects are rudimentary. In most institutions they are adopted from the Government system. What is referred to as performance budget is in fact a simple estimate of income and expenditure for one year. A statement of a few activities accompanies the income and expenditure statements. Its relation to performance is indirect and adds little to the understanding of the budget. Since the Government is the main source of funds the practices of the institutions are geared primarily to the requirements of the Government in this matter. Hence the budget and the statement of income and expenditure show the financial status of various heads of accounts. It is not an instrument of managerial control.

The quantitative index of teaching and research is easy as these activities are individually planned and funded. But no satisfactory index of quality of teaching is available. An index of quality of research is judged from the review of work on publication or by referral. Measures to judge the effectiveness of an institution or to evaluate how well it is serving the purpose are totally inadequate. In some instances review committees are appointed to assess the institution's effectiveness. Some institutions have set up their own committees to review their performance and suggest directions for future. Generally the internal committees have done a more comprehensive and relevant analysis of work than the external committees. The reason for this lies in their styles of working. The internal committees produce serious reports because such reviews are promoted only by institutions which have a comparatively open system. In most cases, however, the decisions on review reports are difficult. The discussion is invariably held on "group" or "faction" lines and not on rational considerations.

In rare cases the changes within the institutions become possible as a result of these reports because internal decision-making is complex and resolution of differences difficult. It is not unusual in most cases to find that the decision-making bodies start a discussion on issues *de novo*, as if no report was available.

The external committees have been less useful because the eminent people appointed to do the job are often unable to give time to understand in depth the problems and issues faced by the institution. The chairman and the secretary do most of the work and drafting of the report with a marginal contribution from other members. While the idea of appointing eminent people is that the committees will be richer by their varied experience, the contribution rarely shows the depth and comprehensiveness that could come if such persons could give their time to this work.

Another reason why committees do not serve the purpose fully is that they review the administrative performance and procedures more than the qualitative aspect of the work of the institution. This kind of review serves a limited purpose.

An effective management information system (MIS) is difficult to develop because of the nature of work carried out in educational and research institutions. Each scientist has a unique or a distinctive contribution to make. The management will need data about his involvement in the institutional tasks, the quality of his input in teaching and in research (the two could be different), and in developing the social system. Since his inputs are distinctive, he must integrate these with the overall teaching and research goals of the institution. Hence, the individual has to be involved in his own task planning, and also that of the institution. The assessment of quality of his input must involve his peers in the subject area, and in related fields. For the MIS the assessment of quality has to be converted into a quantitative index. This measure would have to be sensitive enough to compare the quality of inputs by other scientists in the same, as also in disparate areas.

Little serious work has been done to develop methods to measure the effectiveness of individual activities, or the institution as a whole. Several teaching institutions have been concerned with the measurement of quality of teaching. The various systems used for this purpose are:

1. Student feedback about teaching. This system is used more in Europe and the USA. It is,

however, difficult to establish reliability of the data obtained from such assessment and the objectivity with which the assessment is made.

2. Indirect assessment is made on the basis of the quality of teaching material included in the programme, the injection of new material from one programme to another, the care with which the course is prepared, etc. These measures are based on the premise that if a teacher makes careful preparation, the teaching is likely to be benefit students.
3. The number of students registering for optional courses. This data may show how useful is the course for students. This measure is inadequate because students make the choice of courses for the perceived market demand and not interest alone.

The quality of research output is measured in terms of public review of published papers. If the research findings are not published or are delayed, the assessment of this work is not possible.

A study of the effectiveness of an institution, as discussed earlier, is normally not done (Jackson, 1988). A rough measure used in India is that if the services of an institution are in demand, it must be doing well. The assessment is often made by appointing review committees, but the character of these reports as discussed earlier varies greatly in utility.

This brief review of control and MIS data show that the system is poorly developed. Institutional managements have to rely on their hunches, or assess the situation from bits and pieces of available data. No detailed and systematic analysis of performance is possible because there are a few objective measures available for this purpose. This situation generally exists both in matters of administration and in the areas of core institutional activities, e.g. research and teaching.

The MIS for educational and research institutions is more complex. Research in this area is necessary. The data available at present are primarily "feeling" level data, and depends on the quality of the institutional management. When institutions become large, the assessment of performance in these areas becomes extremely difficult. The assessment of institutional effectiveness is also difficult and a great deal of research is needed to develop objective measures for this purpose. In the absence of reliable measures, the institutional management is as handicapped as the BOG or the public.

(iii) *Organisational Factors*

The work that relies heavily on human skills for quality and results will have to generally involve individuals in decision-making at different levels (Woodward, 1961 and 1969). In high-tech industry close cooperation of the scientist, the technologist and the engineer is necessary (Dayal *et al.*, 1987). In mass production the involvement of employees is comparatively less. In individual-based work systems such as education and research, the involvement of scientists in decision-making, developing open communication and evolving consultative framework are necessary. These systems are unlikely to operate well in an environment of rule-bound legal-rational patterns of administration.

The division of work or a decision to have a departmental or matrix organisation should rest on what is required by work technology. If organisational goals are likely to be achieved by close cooperation between disciplines, as it does in a school of management, for example, the departmental structure will come in the way of effective performance of the task. A school of management will have to have open relationships and scope for mobility for the scientists. Most institutions favour a matrix type of organisation where scientists belong to several groups, each being tied by the task in hand. A departmental structure is easier to administer. Interaction within the department is also easier and more orderly. Decentralisation of administrative authority in a departmental arrangement is also easier. Inter-disciplinary work, however, is more likely to take a formal rather than a natural course. Hence such a pattern could hinder performance which requires inter-disciplinary work. Organisational design has to be consistent with the requirements of the nature of work (technology). The design should facilitate members of a group to set mutually acceptable goals and interact freely to work towards their achievement. The design should also facilitate relations between scientist groups.

(iv) *Institutional Leadership*

The vicious cycle of pro- and counter-manoeuvres, and inability to create rational bases of relationships, often force institutional leaders to deal with affairs as the need arises, even knowing that lack of long-term plans would prevent solution of some of the current problems. Tasks are assigned to those who take them seriously and make the effort to perform them well. Such people interact with the chief executive more often than others who do not take up major responsibility for institutional tasks. These "others" misinterpret this as favouritism and are ever ready to feel aggrieved over trivialities. Often this phenomenon gives rise to what is labelled as the "in-group" and the "out-group". Unwittingly inter-group differences surface — between the groups that is seen to be favoured by the chief executive and the one that is not. Some members of one group at times show partiality for members of the other group and thus inter-group feelings tend to harden. At times, members from the in-group feel disillusioned because they are not given the expected special recognition or favours. Such people often assume aggressive postures. In this kind of social relationship, some persons feel marginalised and neglected. However some members act in a matured way and provide stability to the system. But the social organisation of the institution is tense and small things disturb its tranquillity. The social organisation of a non-hierarchical system is subject to these phenomena more than of the hierarchical. Hence innovative organisations are more open to this kind of social turbulence than the business or more structured organisations.

The institutional leadership is demanding. The research and educational institutions have to be concerned about development of the social environment apart from the administrative system. The social and the work systems have to develop simultaneously. The members of the institution must have pride in achievement and belief in community think. The system needs both the nurturent and the task leadership (Sinha, 1980). Leadership in an innovative organisation cannot rest with one person. It has to be distributive. The reason for this requirement lies in the nature of the work itself. The task has individual orientation. Each person has distinct competence. Take a school of management for example. Peers in the field of one's specialisation can provide leadership, though others would have to raise issues to establish links with related areas and business as a whole. The

Finance, for example, may receive feedback on technical inputs, but production, marketing and other areas will have to point out their interdependence with Finance, and the link with corporate business policy. Three distinct kinds of leadership are necessary in educational and research institutions:

(a) Institutional leadership
(b) Subject leadership
(c) Leadership for social system development.

Institutional leadership has to harmonise and co-ordinate the contribution by subject and social leaders. They have to develop systems that provide autonomy to individuals and groups. Each system has to mature as a discrete or autonomous system and still maintain its links with others. The identity or "think" of such autonomous systems and the total institutions must harmonise. All these aspects have to be promoted more through consent of members and less by authority vested in administrative positions. Deriving from the experience of developing innovative organisations. Chowdhry (1974) has posited that such institutions need a cluster of two or three leaders to flower. She has given examples of the Ahmedabad Textile Industries Research Association (ATIRA), Atomic Energy and Indian Institute of Management, Ahmedabad (IIMA).

The leadership in educational and research institution cannot be provided by a single person, except under specified conditions and for a purpose. The chief executive has an important role to play, but the advice and consent must characterise decision-making. The members of the institution will have to prepare themselves to make both the social and task roles effective. They would have to consciously differentiate their role as individuals, as members of the groups and the community.

Social Organisation

In a developing country trust between and among employees at all levels is extremely rare. This has to be developed consciously. The basic reasons for lack of trust are four:

(i) Lack of consultative and highly mechanistic practices in the organisation.
(ii) Lack of result orientation due to which drift occurs.
(iii) Career progression has almost no link with performance thus preventing factors that help individual motives, integrate with organisational goals.
(iv) Self-centredness of employees and lack of sensitivity for institutional tasks.

The reasons for lack of trust may need further explanation, as both psychological and organisational causes contribute to the phenomenon.

At work many employees unconsciously project childhood reactions to parental authority. In some cases this reaction is one of resentment. In some other cases the reaction is one of total submission and obedience. Only a few are able to establish relationships based on rationality. The first category of people develop resentment for the management. The second category generally operate through an affiliative mode, though in most cases they expect their subordinates to behave in a submissive and obedient manner, thus perpetuating the prevailing styles of interaction in the organisation. The third category accept the reality and discriminate between situations that require agreement and those that invite disagreement.

The supervisors are not comfortable with their supervisory role. They act as middlemen between the higher and the lower levels of employees. The successful middle levels of management supervise through pleading, by building up personalised relationship based on mutual favours but rarely as managers. This situation is further reinforced by trade unions who ignore these levels of employees (Dayal and Sharma, 1976). There is little opportunity of trust and rationality to grow between these levels.

Role-boundary is rarely respected in Indian organisations. There is constant infringement of the boundary of lower positions by higher levels. The middle levels of managers operate in a state of tension, and from one moment to another. In a turbulent environment it is difficult to establish relations of trust. In many cases relations are based on game play — strategy and counter-strategy.

The process of building up viable relationships at all levels of the organisation is a conscious effort. This effort will depend on the nature of interactions between the peers and the hierarchical levels, the autonomy that each sub-unit has and on an individual's concern for results. The management practices should support these efforts. Thus autonomy and de-emphasis on standardisation are necessary conditions to develop viable administrative systems. Viable systems can evolve through experimentation and the institutional management would have to initiate the search for patterns that are most appropriate for them.

The relevant question may be: when education and research institutions in the West do not have to constantly experiment with the social organisation of such institutions, why should it be necessary to do so in India? a detailed discussion on this question may not be necessary here. Three points may, however, be made about most institutions in the West. One, the sub-units of an institution have considerable autonomy to carry out the work independently. The Business School of a University, for example, does its own recruitment, programmes, review and financing. Two, there are minimum rules that are applied to all sub-units and there is little effort to standardise administration. Three, most scientists accept the role-boundary of various administrative bodies and avoid infringement of one by the other. These are in fact broadly the conditions that are necessary for institutions to function well.

9

CONCLUSIONS

In summary, the analysis of organisational processes suggests certain key concerns about managing innovative institutions especially in the context of a developing country. Some of these are summarised below:

1. While external factors influence the internal administrative system, the influence of such factors is substantial when they have receptors within the institution. The impact of standardisation, or rules that are imposed upon the system from another organisation would not be significant, for example, unless the people within the institution felt comfortable with highly structured frame governing their life. Hence external influences are significant to the extent that the ideas or patterns are received favourably by people within the institution. Such patterns get confirmed on account of the support from within the organisation for imposed systems. Rules imposed upon an organisation would not find ready acceptance unless the imposed structure satisfied the need for security and other psychological wants. The donor institution too has a need for *control* which is in some ways satisfied by imposing standardisation. Neither the employees nor the

nisation readily recognise the lity of the rules for the task ss this phenomena is deliberately ie consciousness of both.

hat the ideas or practices are for the task system, as standardisation is to developing on open and interactive social system, the process of changing it would require change among the people within the institution and in the donor organisation alike. While discouraging the donor organisation from imposing standardisation on the host institution, the psychological need of insecurity, rejection and self-centredness among employees would have to be simultaneously handled.

3. Building a democratic system must involve people from within. The involvement has to include a minimum of two aspects: one, adoption or adjustment to the requirement of the task system, and two, participation in decision-making about norms that should govern the life of the work community, i.e. the rule-making function. The first aspect is as important as the second. Handling the second aspect without handling the first would cause interference in the rule-making task. The social system must mature in order to meaningfully participate in the decision-making function. Our knowledge and experience in organisations to develop the social system is extremely limited. Direct experience of changing culture of an organisation is inadequate and a lot more experience in this respect is needed.
4. Organisations have to be seen as a total system. The balance or equilibrium of the system is achieved by all sub-systems exercising different degrees of influence in

different directions. This balance is necessary for a system to remain healthy. Any change in any one sub-system would disturb the balance. Hence, change in the system has to be multi-dimensional. This point has been emphasised in the literature repeatedly but seldom taken note of in problem-solving (Dayal *et al.*, 1981). Consultative practices would have to simultaneously develop a sense of responsibility for the results of the organisation. The administrative and academic systems must be balanced otherwise the stronger will overshadow the weaker and create hostile feelings for the other. Both must develop simultaneously.

5. Leadership is concerned with both decision-making and the dynamics of decision-making, i.e. how best decisions in different aspects are taken. The best decisions are taken where subject knowledge and data are located. It is, therefore, necessary to develop decision-making capabilities at different levels, and at different locations or stations of the organisation. This system is likely to provide greater stability to the organisation than one in which decisions are taken mainly at the top. Democratic organisations would have to develop capabilities for decision-making and problem-solving at different levels of the hierarchy. Such institutions must develop distributive leadership.

BIBLIOGRAPHY

Argyris, C., 1964: *Integrating the Individual and the Organisation.* Wiley, New York.

Brown, W., 1971: *Organisation,* Heinemann, London.

Bernstein, J., 1988: *Three Degrees Above Zero,* Affiliated East-West Press, New Delhi. Interview with Ano Penzias.

Carstairs, G.M., 1957: *The Twice-Born,* Hogarth Press, London.

Chakraborty, S.K., 1987: *Managerial Effectiveness and Quality of Worklife – Indian Insights,* Tata McGraw-Hill, New Delhi.

—–, (ed) 1983: *Board of Directors in India: Their Strategies and Dynamics,* All India Management Association, New Delhi.

Chattopadhyay, P., 1980: Immature Dependency: The problem of Indian Personality in Research Gaps in *Management in Indian Environment,* Chaudhuri, A.K. *et al.* (eds) IIMC Calcutta.

—–, 1975: Dependency in Indian Culture: From Mud Huts to Company Board Rooms, *Indian Management,* Sept-Oct.

—–, 1986: *When the Twin Meet, Western Theory and Eastern Insights in Exploring Indian Organisations,* A.H. Wheeler, Bombay.

Child, J., 1984: New Technologies and Development in Management Organisation, *Journal of Management Science,* Vol. 12, No. 3, pp. 211-224.

Chowdhry, K., 1972: *Change-in-Organisations*, Vikas, New Delhi.

Crozier, M., 1964: *The Bureaucratic Phenomenon*, University of Chicago Press, Chicago, p. 94.

Dayal, I., 1988: Organisation of IIM, Lucknow, Paper prepared for South Asian Round Table, March 1-5, *Mimeograph*, IIM, Lucknow.

—, *et al.*, 1987: Managing High Technology, *Monography*, IIM, Lucknow.

—, 1981: Concept of Man in Management, *Economic and Political Weekly*, Vol. XVI, No. 22, pp. M81-M-87.

Dayal, I., 1977: *Change in Work Organisation*, Concept, New Delhi.

—, 1976: Cultural Factors in Designing Performance Appraisal Systems, *Vikalpa*, Vol. 1, No. 2, 1976.

—, 1967: Constraints of Legislation on Organisational. Effectiveness, *Indian Journal of Industrial Relations*, Vol. 2, No. 3.

Dayal, I., and Dayal, A.K., 1983: *Organisation for Management in Developing Countries* (Second Edition), Concept, New Delhi.

Dayal, I., and Sharma, B.R., 1976: *Management of Trade Unions*, Shri Ram Centre, New Delhi.

Dayal, I., Mathur, K. and Bhattacharya, M., 1975: *District Administration*, Macmillan,. New Delhi.

Drucker, P.F., 1988: Management and the World's Work, *Harvard Business Review*, (Sept-Oct.) pp. 65-70.

Friedman, G., 1955: *Industrial Society*, The Free Press of Glencoe, New York.

Garret, J., 1972: *The Management of Government*, Pelican, U.K.

Homans, G.C., 1950: *The Human Group*, Harcourt, Brace, New York.

Kakar, S., 1971: Rationality and Irrationality in Business Leadership, *Journal Business Policy*, Vol. 2, No. 2.

—, 1970: Authority Patterns and Subordinate Behaviour in Indian Organisations, IIM, Ahmedabad, Mimeograph.

Mahindra, A., 1980: Management, *Business India*, Oct. 31, p. 48.

McGregar, D., 1966: Leadership and Motivation, M.I.T. Press, Cambridge, Mass.

—, 1960: *The Human Side of Enterprise*, McGraw-Hill, New York.

Merton, R.K., 1957: *Bureaucratic Structure and Personality in Social Theory and Social Structure*, Free Press of Glencoe, New York.

—, 1952: *Reader in Bureaucracy*, Free Press of Glencoe, Illinois.

Miller, E.J. and Rice, A.K., 1967: *Systems of Organisation*, Tavistock, London.

Mouzeles, N.P., 1967: *Organisation and Bureaucracy*, Routledge and Kegan Paul, London.

Rice, A.K., 1970: *The Modern University*, Tavistock, London.

Saxena, A.P., 1990: *Nehru on Administration*, Uppal Publishing, New Delhi.

Sinha J.B.P., 1977: the Quality of Working Life in the Indian Setting, *Journal of Social and Economic Studies* 5(2), pp. 235-248.

—, 1974: the Psycho-Social Background and Work Motivation in S.K. Roy and A.S. Menon (eds.) *Motivation and Organisational Effectiveness*, SRC Industrial Relations and Human Resources, New Delhi, pp. 1-28

Trist, E.L. *et al.*, 1963: *Organisational Choice*, Tavistock, London.

Trist, E.L. and Bamforth, K.W., 1951: Some Social and Psychological Consequences of the Longwell

Method of Coat-getting, *Human Relations*, pp. 3-38.

Vroom, V.H. & Yetton, P.W., 1973: *Leadership and Decision-making*, University of Pittsburgh Press, Pittsburgh.

Walker, C.R., 1962: *Modern Technology and Civilisation*, McGraw-Hill, New York.

Whiting, B., 1968: *Six Cultures — Studies of Child Rearing*, Wiley, New York.

Whyte, W.F., 1969: *Organisational Behaviour, Theory and Application*, Irwin-Darsey, Homewood, Illinois.

—, 1959: Man, in Organisation, Richard D. Irwin, Homewood, Illinois.

Woodward J. (ed), 1970: *Organisation and Productivity*, Oxford University Press, London.

—, 1965: *Industrial Organisation: Theory and Practice*, Oxford University, Press, London.

INDEX